CANADIAN PEACEKEEPERS

Ten Stories of Valour in War-Torn Countries

Norman S. Leach

FOLK
LORE
PUBLISHING

The Publisher: Folklore Publishing

Website: www.folklorepublishing.com

Library and Archives Canada Cataloguing in Publication

Leach, Norman, 1963–
    Canadian peacekeepers : Ten stories of valour in war-torn countries / Norman S. Leach

(Great Canadian Stories series)
Includes bibliographic references.
ISBN 1-894864-36-0

    1. Peacekeeping forces—Canada—Biography. 2. Canada. Canadian Armed Forces—Biography. 3. Peacekeeping forces—Canada—History. I. Title. II. Series

JZ6377.C3L42 2005   355.3'57'092271   C2005-902138-1

Project Director: Faye Boer
Project Editor: Terry McIntyre
Production: Trina Koscielnuk
Cover Design: Valentino

Cover Image: Roméo Dallaire; Courtesy of the National Defence Imagery Library, ISC94-2114.

We acknowledge the support of the Alberta Foundation for the Arts for our publishing program.

PC:P6

Contents

Dedication

To my wife Maritza and my daughter Stephanie.
Thank you for your support.

~⋈~

Acknowledgements

The author recognizes the dedication and sacrifices made by Canada's peacekeepers throughout the years. This book is written out of respect for all those who have served our country.

~⋈~

Introduction

The UN, Canada and Peacekeeping

FOR MOST CANADIANS THE TRENCHES OF WORLD WAR I AND the World War II battlefields of Europe and the Pacific are not just distant memories—they are ancient history. For many today it is hard to believe that when the Empire called, Canada answered. From the Boer War to World War II entire generations of young men fought and died in foreign lands protecting their families, their country and freedom.

When asked, most Canadian schoolchildren would say that Canada is a peaceful country—with no real military past. In fact, Canadians in general would probably answer that Canada is a peace-loving country and that its commitment to the United Nations (UN) and peacekeeping defines it as a nation. Canadians feel they invented peace-keeping—and in a way they are right.

According to the UN's long-standing definition, peacekeeping is: "the deployment of international military and civilian personnel to a conflict area with the consent of the parties in order to: stop or contain hostilities or supervise the carrying out of a peace agreement."

When the UN was formed in 1945, Canada felt that the greatest strength of the UN Charter was that it would, for the very first time, extend the rule of law to the entire world. The Charter would give nations a way to settle disputes and to control violence. Ironically, the Charter gave the UN the right to use collective military force to maintain peace.

However, the decades-long Cold War between the Soviet Union and the West meant that the UN Security Council was never able to agree on just how to maintain peace. Both the United States and the Soviet Union held vetoes at the Security Council so neither was willing to agree to a UN military action in their sphere of influence. This left the UN as the proverbial dog with a big bark—but no bite.

UN military observers were only allowed to watch the movements of armies, supervise cease-fires, work with local citizens and generally encourage peace. From the start, in April 1948, Canada participated by providing eight officers for the UN mission to Kashmir and then sent another four officers to the Arab-Israeli borders as part of the Palestine mission in May of the same year. To the amazement of everyone the missions were generally successful.

In June 1950 a crisis flared up in the Korean peninsula. North Korean forces moved into the South, almost unopposed. Soon the South Korean army was in full retreat, and Seoul fell in early July. The only territory held by the South Koreans—and a small force of Americans—was in the deep south near the city of Pusan. American supplies and air support allowed the South Korean forces to maintain a tenuous hold on the area, but the North Koreans threatened to overrun them at any time.

At that time, the USSR was boycotting the Security Council because the UN refused to allow Mongolia to join as a full member. This meant the Soviet Union would not be at the Security Council table to veto any resolutions. The U.S. used the opening to organize an international "police action" under UN control to push the North Koreans back.

The UN command ultimately consisted of 272,000 South Koreans and 266,000 from the other 16 nations who supported the action. Altogether 26,791 Canadians served in Korea and 516 gave their lives. Canada, consistent with her history, made a proportionally larger contribution than most of the nations who served in Korea.

Three years later, in July 1953, the "police action" came to an end. While North and South Korea agreed to a ceasefire, it was really the UN that won. It proved that it could live up to its ideals of peacekeeping—if given the chance.

The police action in Korea was not typical. UN peacekeepers were not usually asked to enforce ceasefires or international agreements by force of arms. Their only real offensive weapons were the authority of the UN and the support of the UN's member nations. As defined by the UN's original mandate, a solution cannot be imposed on unwilling parties.

Today, the UN endorses two main types of peacekeeping. United Nations Military Observers, known as UNMOs are sent to observe and report on a negotiated truce. Generally unarmed, the UN observers count on their presence and moral suasion to carry the day. The UNMO's openly report any violations they see over unencrypted radio, ensuring both sides know just what the other has done. The UNMO's also ensure the world press sees their reports both in the country itself and at UN Headquarters in New York.

The UN can also call on combat units to patrol the ceasefire zones as agreed to by the warring factions. By placing armed, professional and neutral troops between the combatants, the UN works to ensure the stability of the ceasefire. Many ceasefire operations call for both UNMO and armed peacekeepers.

Peacekeeping is not for the faint of heart. The qualities that make a good combat soldier do not necessarily make a good peacekeeper. According to the experts: "Peacekeepers today must be effective negotiators, be capable of standing firm in the face of hostile forces, and be prepared to endure privation. As demands on peacekeepers increase, so too must the skills required to meet them."

UN peacekeeping operations in the late 1990s and into the new millennium have included:

making peace, disarming combatants, de-mining operations, leading humanitarian convoys and even organizing elections. Canadian peacekeepers have worked with local authorities to provide expertise in everything from law, media, health and tax administration to the management of infrastructure.

Since 1956, more than 750,000 military troops and police have served as UN peacekeepers. However, when the Cold War ended, the UN was faced with a new series of challenges. Between 1991 and the end of 1996, the UN set up 24 new peacekeeping missions. In the first 43 years of peacekeeping, they had set up only 37. In the mid-1990s nearly 80,000 international peacekeepers were serving in hotspots from the Balkans to the Middle East to Central America. More than 100,000 Canadians have participated in UN and NATO peacekeeping missions and over 100 have given their lives protecting not only global freedom but also the lives of innocents.

The Suez Crisis:
The First United Nations
Emergency Force

BY 1955 BRITAIN WAS COMMITTED TO ENDING ITS
colonization of Asia and Africa and gave up con-
trol of the vital Suez Canal to the Egyptian govern-
ment of Gamal Abdel Nasser. The following year,
Britain refused Nasser's request for financial sup-
port for the Aswan High Dam on the Nile. Nasser
ordered the Suez Canal be nationalized and told a
cheering crowd that the imperialists could "choke
on their rage."

In October 1956, a joint British, French and
Israeli force attempted to seize the canal. First, the
Israelis launched an attack against Egypt causing
the Egyptians to respond in force. Israel then asked
Britain and France for assistance in the face of the
much larger Egyptian army. The invasion sparked
an international crisis forcing the UN to act.

CHAPTER ONE

The Founder: Lester B. Pearson
(1897–1972)

LESTER B. PEARSON WOULD COME TO SYMBOLIZE CANADA TO Canadians and the world. Whether in diplomacy or politics, "Mike" was able to reach out to others and find solutions that were as elegant as they were simple.

But there was really no indication that Lester B. Pearson was marked for greatness. Born in April 1897, his father and mother were both from Toronto and descendants of solid Irish families, but there the similarity ended. Lester's father was a conservative Methodist minister, while his mother was liberal in both her political and life views.

Lester was 16 years old when he was admitted to Victoria College, at the University of Toronto, where he shared a residence room in Gate House with his brother Duke. Lester was soon making a name for himself as an athlete—both in ice hockey and rugby.

In 1914 the world was plunged into war when the Archduke Ferdinand was assassinated in Sarajevo. Lester, like many young men of his generation, decided to interrupt his studies and go to

Europe to fight the Hun. He was too young to enlist in the regular army, but Lester soon found a solution. A friend sent a message to him that the University of Toronto was sponsoring a hospital unit, and there was one space left. Lester ran all the way to the recruiting station and volunteered—he was on his way to Europe.

Lester spent the next two years in England, Egypt and Greece (where his unit fought against the Bulgarians). Working in a hospital, Lester saw all the horrors of the war first-hand, but he believed it was a just cause.

When he turned 18, Lester was commissioned as an officer and immediately transferred to the Royal Flying Corps (RFC). It was while he was learning to fly that his flight instructor decided that the name "Lester" was just not manly enough for an officer in the RFC! Lester was rechristened "Mike"—a nickname that remained with him for the rest of his life.

Pearson was sent to hospital in England after sustaining injuries in two accidents—including a plane crash. However, he was not returned to Toronto until after he was run over by a London City bus while on leave. In Toronto, after he had recovered, he returned to active duty training new pilots while he continued his university studies at night.

When the armistice was signed in 1919, Mike finished his studies and received a BA from the

University of Toronto. Like many young men who had survived the war, Mike found it hard to settle down. A career seemed a long way from flying fighters over France.

He first tried law but soon thought that he was better suited to business. For two years he worked for Armour and Company, a meat-processing firm, although he never really fitted in. His stint at Armour would come up years later. Mike was working at the UN when the Russians accused him of once working for an armament manufacturer!

Unfortunately, Mike was really no more success-ful in business than he had been in law, and he eventually returned to academic life, winning a two-year fellowship at Oxford University. He earned a BA in modern history in 1923 and an MA in 1925. He also returned to the sporting life, win-ning his "blues" (an award that recognized excel-lence) in both lacrosse and ice hockey.

He soon returned to his alma mater and became a professor in the history department. It was a busy year. Mike coached football and played tennis on the U of T team. He also somehow found time to court and eventually marry Maryon Moody of Toronto, in 1925. The couple had two children—a daughter and a son.

Pearson was a member of the working poor—trying to raise a family on a professor's salary. Looking for new opportunities—and more money—he resigned his position at the U of T and in 1928 joined the Canadian Department of External Affairs as first secretary.

The work at external affairs fit both Mike's personality and his skills. The deputy minister, O.D. Skelton, noted that Mike was a "perceptive observer and an able writer"—both skills that would serve him well his entire career.

Pearson became a regular in international diplomatic circles. In 1930 he participated in the Hague Conference on Codification of International Law. The following year he was loaned as secretary to a commission on wheat futures; in both 1933 and 1934 he was a delegate to the Geneva World Disarmament Conference, then sent to the London Naval Conference of 1935, and finally, to sessions of the League of Nations at the end of that same year. It had been a busy seven years—and a steep learning curve.

From 1935 to 1941 he was appointed to serve at the High Commission for Canada in London. From there, Mike could see the gathering storm clouds in Europe. He also had access to the halls of power—and to the men who would fight the coming war and make history. It was here that he developed his belief that if the world were to survive, it would need to mount a collective defence against both dictators and aggression.

With his time in London completed, Mike returned to Canada in 1941 and assumed the role of assistant undersecretary of state for external affairs at Ottawa. His rise would not end there. In June 1942, he was promoted to minister-counsellor at the Canadian Legation, in Washington. Mike's charm soon won over both the diplomatic corps and media alike. Ottawa recognized a success when it saw it, and in July 1944, Mike was made the minister plenipotentiary and finally, in January 1945, he was named Canada's ambassador to the United States. Lester "Mike" Pearson had arrived.

While in Washington, in 1943, Mike was one of the Canadian representatives to the commission that would ultimately establish the United Nations Relief and Rehabilitation Administration (UNRRA) and the UN Food and Agriculture Organization (FAO). In 1944 Mike attended the Dumbarton Oaks Conference to discuss the potential of establishing an organization of united nations and the San Francisco conference on the establishment of the UN in 1945.

The San Francisco conference, attended by 50 countries, met to draw up the UN Charter. The 50 member countries signed the document on June 26, 1945, and the UN officially came into existence on October 24, 1945, when China, France, the Soviet Union, the United Kingdom (UK) and the United States (U.S.) ratified the San Francisco Agreement.

Pearson had been noticed at the highest levels of the House of Commons in Ottawa. Prime Minister Mackenzie King ordered him home, and in the fall of 1946, named him deputy minister (or undersec-retary) of external affairs. Mike's attention—driven by the politics of the day—was focused on increasing the political and economic ties between Canada's post-war allies the U.S. and the UK.

While Mike still believed in the UN, he also remembered his wartime experiences in London and worked to develop a Western defensive alliance to counteract the Soviet Union. Mike drafted the speech that was delivered by Prime Minister Louis St. Laurent, who had replaced the retired Mackenzie King in 1948, in which the new prime minister proposed the establishment of the North Atlantic Treaty Organization (NATO).

However, by the time the NATO proposal was being seriously considered in world capitals, Pearson had moved on to new challenges. The Liberal Party of Canada was going into a general election in 1948, and it convinced the popular bureaucrat to run in the riding of Algoma East, in Ontario. When the ballots were counted, Canada had a new MP, and Mike Pearson had a new career.

Prime Minister St. Laurent rewarded Mike for his victory by naming the rookie parliamentarian to the position of minister of external affairs in September 1948. It was a position Mike was to hold until the Liberal government was defeated by the Conservative government of John Diefenbaker, nine years later.

Mike Pearson had come full circle. The consummate bureaucrat, who had proposed Canada becoming part of NATO and who had encouraged his prime minister to join the alliance, was now the elected representative of the Government of Canada who signed the NATO-enabling treaty in 1949, led the Canadian delegation to NATO until 1957 and was chairman of the NATO Council in 1951–52.

Pearson was assigned other responsibilities as well. The prime minister asked him to lead the Canadian delegation at the UN from 1946 to 1956, and he was elected as the President of the General Assembly in 1952–53. He was also to serve as the Chairman of the General Assembly's Special Committee on Palestine and led efforts to establish the state of Israel in 1947.

True to his vision of a united front against tyranny, Mike worked to have Canada participate militarily in the UN police action in Korea. Fighting the battle on two fronts, he also tried to find a political solution for the region. The Americans were not pleased with the Canadian president of the General Assembly; accusing him of giving in on too many points, especially the most difficult, during negotiations.

When Egyptian President Gamal Abdel Nasser seized the Suez Canal and nationalized it in 1956, the UK, France and Israel combined forces in an effort to take it back. For a time, the world teetered on the brink of at least a regional war—if not another world war—with those in the Soviet and U.S. camps taking sides in the conflict. The Suez Crisis became the focus of world attention.

On November 1, 1956, the UN General Assembly met in an emergency session and passed a resolution condemning the three allies in the invasion. The Assembly itself faced a crisis when the U.S. demanded an immediate ceasefire. The Assembly was clearly divided on political lines—mostly based on Cold War alliances. Mike faced a larger challenge. Since World War II, the U.S. had become Canada's largest trading partner and was vital to Canadian defence. On the other hand, support from Canada for the U.S. position would antagonize Britain and France—and their considerable numbers of supporters at home in Canada.

Further, Mike knew that a ceasefire would be ineffective if the UN was neither ready—nor able—to supervise and support it. Mike, realizing he was in a no-win situation, abstained from the vote on the US resolution, mostly to buy himself some more time.

When Mike faced the (now-divided) UN General Assembly, he made the case that a ceasefire would not meet the goals of either side. "In six months, we'll go through all this again if we do not take advantage of this crisis...to do something about a political settlement." Mike's solution involved creating a special emergency force to keep peace on the Israeli-Egyptian border once an agreement was reached by all the parties.

Everyone involved recognized that Mike's plan was the only one that had any hope of success. On November 4, the UN voted to accept the Pearson Peacekeeping proposal. The United Nations Emergency Force (UNEF) was established, with Canadian General E.L.M. Burns as its commander. For the first time in its history, the UN had a true peacekeeping force.

True to his beliefs, Mike knew that Canadian soldiers had to be represented—in force—in the UNEF. On November 2, 1956, he declared, "We need action not only to end the fighting but to make the peace. My own government would be glad to recommend Canadian participation in such a United Nations force, a truly international peace and police force." By mid-November, advance units of the Canadian military contingent began to arrive in the Suez Canal zone.

The Canadian government agreed to send the 1st Battalion of The Queen's Own Rifles (QOR) of Canada, an infantry unit with a long history and an exemplary service record as a steady and experienced force. They seemed the perfect choice for the volatile assignment in Egypt. The QOR, with its vehicles and equipment, was ordered to move from its base in Calgary to Halifax, for shipment to the Middle East. The men were on board the HMCS *Magnificent* when word came that the QOR would not be going to Egypt. President Nasser refused to accept a regiment of "soldiers of the Queen" as part of the UN force.

To Nasser and the Egyptians, the QOR's name and uniforms and the then Canadian flags appeared to be simply copies of those of the British invaders. Egyptian officials argued that their appearance in the volatile war zone would inflame passions, not cool them down. The Canadians backed down and agreed that rather than infantry troops, Canada would provide communications and logistics troops. They would ensure the fighting forces remained effective by delivering critical supplies and were deemed just as important as infantry.

Pearson later claimed that his experience in Egypt was a driving force in his commitment to Canada eventually having its own flag.

Canadian combat troops eventually served in the UNEF. When it was decided that the UNEF needed a reconnaissance unit, it turned to Yugoslavia and Canada to provide the necessary forces. The Royal Canadian Dragoons and Lord Strathcona's Horse initially provided men, Ferret scout cars and jeeps. Over time, Canada would also commit reconnaissance squadrons from the Fort Garry Horse and the 8th Canadian Hussars.

The peacekeepers of the UNEF supervised the withdrawal of the British, French and Israeli forces and acted as a buffer between Egypt and Israel, thereby maintaining the peace. In 1967 Egypt forced the UN forces to leave, but they would return. In 1973 a second UNEF mission was established, lasting six more years.

International recognition followed the peacekeepers' success in Egypt. In 1957 Mike won the Nobel Peace Prize for his leadership in creating the UN force. The world media declared him the father of modern peacekeeping, but international acclaim came at domestic cost.

Pearson and the St-Laurent government were widely blamed for not standing by Britain and France—the mother countries—during the Suez Crisis. When a general election was called, in 1957, the Liberals went down to defeat, and Prime Minister St-Laurent resigned as leader.

Mike was the natural successor to St-Laurent and was elected leader by the party in 1958, defeating Paul Martin Sr. Mike inherited the Liberal Party when it was at an all-time low. The Conservatives, under John Diefenbaker, had a minority government and seemed ready to rule. Injudiciously, in his first act as Leader of the Opposition, Mike dared Diefenbaker to hand over government to the Liberals or call an election. Diefenbaker called an election and won the largest majority in Canadian electoral history. Mike was left with only 49 of the 265 seats in the House of Commons. He had his work cut out for him.

Pearson worked tirelessly to revive the near-dead Liberal Party. In the 1962 general election, his leadership allowed the party to win a total of 100 seats. In 1963 the Diefenbaker government announced that it would be willing to allow nuclear weapons on Canadian soil as part of its commitment to North American defence. The Canadian public disagreed, and in the spring of 1963, Mike and the Liberals formed a minority government with 128 seats.

On April 22, 1963, Mike sat in the prime minister's chair for the first time. He took office with Canadians hoping that his government would lead with the professionalism that had marked his international career. In fact, Mike could not control parliament, and bickering and infighting marred his first term. When he called an election in 1965, Mike won, but again with a minority government.

As prime minister, Pearson never had a majority in the House of Commons. However, he never lost sight of what he believed were the Canadian ideals. On domestic issues, his government implemented new directions in old age pensions, medical care, governmental assistance for higher education and technical and vocational education; the redistribution of electoral districts and reformation of legislative procedures. And before retiring, he oversaw Canada's 1967 centennial celebrations and also introduced a new Canadian flag.

The federal Liberal government followed a bipartisan foreign policy based on a philosophy of internationalism. Mike stood against American involvement in Vietnam and refused to participate in the South-East Asia conflict. When he spoke at Temple University, Philadelphia, Pennsylvania, in 1965 he declared Canada's support for a negotiated settlement to the war. Later, he was a guest at the Texas ranch of U.S. President Lyndon Johnson. Johnson reportedly grabbed Pearson by the lapels and shook the Canadian Prime Minister in absolute frustration.

The Pearson Cabinet of 1965 was to leave a legacy well beyond its policies, victories and defeats. Three of Canada's future prime ministers served under and learned from Mike Pearson— Pierre Trudeau, John Turner and Jean Chrétien.

Pearson decided to end his political career in December 1967. At the April 1968 Liberal Convention, he passed control on to the new prime minister, Pierre Elliott Trudeau.

Coming full circle, Mike Pearson, Nobel Prize winner and former prime minister, returned to teaching, this time international relations at Carleton University in Ottawa. But public life was never far away for him. In 1968 he was appointed to head a commission sponsored by the International Bank for Reconstruction and Development to review and plan the future of economic aid to developing countries. Also in 1968 Canada recognized Mike Pearson's decades of public service by making him a Companion of the Order of Canada.

Lester B. "Mike" Pearson died of cancer in Ottawa on December 27, 1972, and was buried in the nearby Gatineau Hills in the MacLaren Cemetery, Wakefield, Québec.

Lester B. Pearson will always be remembered as the founder of modern peacekeeping, but his name lives on in other ways in Canada. In 1984, Pierre Elliott Trudeau renamed Toronto International Airport as Pearson International Airport. Other named places are: the Lester B. Pearson College in Victoria, BC; Lester B. Pearson School Board in Montréal; and National Hockey League's Lester B. Pearson Award to the most valuable player, as judged by his peers. Mike's favourite sport was baseball, and the Pearson Cup has honoured the winner of an annual contest between the Montréal Expos and the Toronto Blue Jays.

In 1994, the Canadian government established the Lester B. Pearson Canadian International Peacekeeping Training Centre. The centre, located on a former military base in Clementsport, Nova Scotia, provides research, education and training for peacekeepers from Canada and abroad.

The *New York Times* of December 30, 1972, said of Pearson:

His skill as negotiator and mediator during and after World War II enabled Canada to play a world role out of proportion to its size and power. His contributions to launching of the United Nations and the Atlantic Alliance were creative and enduring. This phase of Mr. Pearson's public life was climaxed by his heroic part in defusing the Suez Crisis of 1956 that might have exploded in World War III. He richly deserved the Nobel Peace Prize, awarded in 1957 for his initiative in establishing the UN Emergency Force in Gaza.

CHAPTER TWO

E.L.M. Burns
(1897–1985)

EASON LOUIS MILLARD BURNS WAS BORN IN WESTMONT, Québec, on June 17, 1897, although he would never be known as Eason. For all of his life—and to everyone he met—he was simply Tommy, a childhood nickname.

The Canadian, who would eventually command the first United Nations Peacekeeping Force, found himself at The Royal Military College in Kingston, Ontario in 1915 when World War I broke out. Like many of his peers, 17-year-old Tommy chafed to go "over there." As soon as he turned 18, he received a special War Certificate and immediately joined the Royal Canadian Engineers as a signaller.

Sent first to England and then France, Tommy was soon on the front lines—seeing the war up close. Over the next two years, he was wounded twice and also won the Military Cross (MC) for laying and repairing communications lines while under enemy fire. When the war ended 20-year-old Tommy Burns was a staff captain with the 12th Infantry Brigade—the youngest staff captain in the British Empire's armies in France.

At the close of the war it was obvious to everyone that Tommy would make a career for himself in the army. So, it was no surprise that he enlisted with the Engineers Corps of the Canadian Permanent Force. He was soon lecturing at the Royal Military College, his alma mater. He earned a reputation as a brilliant lecturer and writer, even entering an essay he wrote for the Bertrand Stewart prize. Tommy won the prize—one coveted by those across the empire.

Burns studied at the School of Military Engineering, at Chatham, England, in 1920–21. While there he mastered French and German, enabling him to read scientific works in their source languages.

Finding his studies not challenging enough, he began working with the well-known writer, Madge MacBeth, with the aim of writing several novels—just as a hobby. He also contributed regular articles to well-known magazines, such as *Canadian Defence Quarterly* and the *American Mercury,* under the pen name of Arlington B. Conway. His articles covered topics as diverse as the training of troops and the bombing of large cities.

In 1927, Tommy wrote the entrance exams for the prestigious British Staff College at Quetta, India. He obtained admission for the 1928–29 school year by receiving the highest marks among all the competitors from the United Kingdom, India, the Dominions and the Colonies.

Burns received the Order of the British Empire (OBE) in 1937 for his inventions in the area of radial stereoplotters and multiplex aeroprojectors, while he was in charge of the geographical section of the Canadian General Staff. A newspaper reporter in Ottawa described Tommy Burns as "the brain that marches like a soldier." The phrase stuck for the rest of his career.

An outstanding soldier, Tommy was soon promoted to major in 1927, receiving a lieutenant colonel's brevet (a temporary rank) in 1935 and was a lieutenant colonel by 1939. After 20 years of peacetime soldiering and studying, Lieutenant Colonel E.L.M. Burns, O.B.E., M.C., was selected as one of the few Canadians ever to study at the Imperial Defence College in London, England.

When war broke out, in September 1939, Tommy's superiors thought he was a brilliant officer destined for command. His fellow officers at the Defence College had another view, describing him as "not a natural leader, but he knows exactly what he is talking about and exactly what he is doing."

The Canadian government ordered Burns to suspend his studies at the Imperial Defence College and focus both on establishing a Canadian military headquarters in London and preparing for the reception of the 1st Canadian Infantry Division. Tommy did so well he was made a full colonel in May 1940. His knowledge and experience made him the perfect choice as assistant deputy chief of the general staff in Ottawa.

In 1941, Tommy returned to England as brigadier general, general staff, at corps headquarters. The next year he was promoted to major general and returned to Canada to organize the Canadian Armoured Corps. He was being groomed for a top position and was given command of both the 4th Canadian Armoured Brigade and 2nd Canadian Infantry Division and then the 5th Canadian Armoured Division in England.

By March 1944, Tommy Burns was a lieutenant general in command of the 1st Canadian Corps in Italy, breaking through the German lines in the Liri Valley. In September the 1st Canadian Corps crushed the Gothic Line in Rimini allowing the Allies access to all of northern Italy.

Canadian newspapers were calling Tommy "Burns of Italy," as if he was winning the war in Italy all by himself. However, just like at the Defence College, his colleagues believed otherwise. He became known to his troops as "Smiler" Burns because Tommy never seemed to smile.

Tommy's superiors and subordinates were quickly losing confidence in the general who seemed unable to give inspired leadership. When new army commanders arrived in Italy, Burns' divisional commanders convinced the British officers that the victories in Italy had been in spite of Burns—not because of him.

Soon there were calls for the Canadian government to remove Burns from command. Giving in to the demands, the government demoted Tommy to major general, and he was transferred behind the lines as General Officer Commanding, Canadian Section, General Headquarters, 2nd Echelon, 21 Army Group—a purely administrative post.

Although he was awarded the Distinguished Service Order (DSO), Tommy's four-year meteoric rise through four ranks was at its wartime end. Burns seemed a failure despite his renowned genius.

Tommy Burns, the professional soldier, called it quits and retired in 1947. He left behind over 30 years in the army. Tommy accepted a post at the Department of Veteran Affairs in Ottawa. However, his luck seemed to have returned. In 1949 he was selected as an alternative representative on the Canadian delegation to the United Nations General Assembly. His time at the UN gave him a solid international and political understanding, preparing him for the post of Deputy Minister of Veterans Affairs, a post he held from 1950 to 1954.

In 1954, Canada was asked to provide a commander for the United Nations Truce Supervision Organization (UNTSO), a peacekeeping unit at the Israeli-Arab border. The Government of Canada turned to Tommy, asking him to accept the post. His years in the military and government made him the perfect choice to command a peacekeeping force fraught with tension and intrigue.

An international incident exploded in Egypt in 1956. When Egyptian President Nasser nationalized the Suez Canal Israel, Britain and France tried to reclaim the canal by force. Military intervention in Egypt threatened to plunge the world back into war with Cold War allies aligned on opposite sides.

Canada's Lester B. Pearson led the negotiations that established the United Nations Emergency Force (UNEF) in November 1956. Pearson won a Nobel Prize for convincing the world that putting neutral military forces between the two opposing sides would be a way to ensure that the negotiated ceasefire held. It was a good idea but was missing an important ingredient—without the right leadership, the peacekeeping plan was doomed to failure.

Once again, the Canadian government turned to Lieutenant General "Tommy" Burns. Tommy was available, and with his UNTSO experience in both the politics and logistical problems of the region, he was the perfect choice. Speaking about the early days of the mission and how well Pearson and Burns worked together, J. King Gordon, public relations officer on the UNEF staff, said, "Pearson's reputation for peacekeeping could not have been gained without this partnership."

On November 8, 1956, Tommy Burns flew into Cairo on the first aircraft allowed into the airport previously bombed by the British. His job was to work with President Nasser to establish a working agreement that would allow the peacekeeping force to carry out its duties.

Like Pearson, Burns quickly had to come to grips with the make up of the Canadian contingent. The Queen's Own Rifles (QOR) unit of Calgary was ready to leave for Egypt and UNEF service. President Nasser protested that the people of Egypt would not welcome the QOR, with their British name and uniforms. He claimed that he could not guarantee the Canadian soldiers' safety.

Falling back on his administrative experience gained in Europe, Burns knew that more than enough combat troops had been committed to the UN force. What was really needed was administrative staff to look after communications, transport, supply and air reconnaissance. Nasser agreed and soon Canadians were "directing traffic" in Egypt.

The Danes and Norwegians arrived in Egypt on November 15. Burns, quickly grasping the severity of the situation, ordered them to Port Said. Tommy recognized that though the British and French had caused a great loss of life and physical damage in the area, the international force of neutral Danes and Norwegians would go a long way to stabilizing the region—and would be a much-needed success for the UN.

The next order of business was to negotiate the withdrawal of the French and British. Burns, at the direction of the UN Secretary-General, negotiated directly with the commanders of the respective countries. A timetable for withdrawal was established with both the French and British commanders asking for one month to remove all of their forces and equipment. Burns agreed, and the two European countries made their exit on December 22, 1956.

It was a different scenario with the Israelis, who were in no rush to abandon Gaza. On January 14, 1957, a Yugoslav contingent to the UNEF took over El'Arish when the Israelis evacuated it. There the withdrawal stalled.

The Israelis refused to leave Rafah, at the far southern end of the Gaza Strip, wanting assurances that the UNEF would occupy and administer Gaza. Tommy personally handled the negotiations, driving up from his headquarters to deal directly with the Israelis. However, even Tommy could not force the Israeli forces to leave Gaza. Finally, the Israelis agreed to withdraw, according to the terms of the General Assembly resolution, following pressure from the UN and the United States. However, even then there was a delay of several days.

The delay was almost more than Burns could stand. His staff knew that he liked to be in control; many described him as very quiet and orderly at the best of times. None of them had ever seen him so frustrated and annoyed. But peacekeeping was different from waging war. All he could do was wait until the Israelis were ready to move. Finally,

Burns and his forces moved into Gaza on the night of March 6–7.

It was evident to everyone around him that Burns enjoyed working with the diverse nationalities of the UNEF. When asked, he would later claim that working with the 6000 troops was not as complicated as it seemed. Several of the senior officers had attended the same staff colleges, and there was a common understanding of how to do things.

Gordon later wrote:

Above all this, Burns was a highly professional military man, and he carried enormous respect. He happened to know the situation inside out; he had great intelligence and also great curiosity, and he made a point of discovering the political situation behind everything. He was not simply the military commander; he was also a political figure, representative of Dag Hammarskjöld, the UN Secretary-General.

Burns faced the challenge of deploying 6000 men over a large area of desert. As a foreshadowing of missions yet to come, the UNEF was short of transportation. To solve the problem, Tommy went to the British commanders and agreed to buy some of their trucks and supplies. It was a win-win situation. The UN got its transport, and the British could withdraw that much faster not having to load the trucks.

As the Israelis withdrew, they destroyed the roads behind them, rendering Tommy's new trucks useless. Burns ordered the roads rebuilt. He faced logistics problems in feeding his troops. The Indian contingent was not happy with what the Danes and Norwegians were eating and vice versa. Such were the challenges of peacekeeping in a modern world!

Burns quickly realized that peacekeeping would only work when it held the world's attention. Bringing his international press liaisons together, he ordered that a newspaper be produced to tell the story of the peacekeeping force. Burns even chose the title—*The Sand Dune*. Tommy was comfortable with various writers who were contributing both local and international stories. After all, he had been a writer in his university days. But *The Sand Dune* was a propaganda tool, and Burns made sure it was read at the UN headquarters in New York. The newspaper had a wide audience and helped solidify the force in Egypt.

The UN was learning what made a peacekeeping operation work. The success of Tommy Burns' mission would depend on having a firm agreement between the parties to the dispute backed by the large powers in the world. Once those elements were in place, the mission required solid administration and execution under the leadership of an experienced person—Tommy was the right person at the right time.

Gordon later wrote:

In this case, with the exception of the Israeli delay over evacuating Gaza, all these factors were positive. You have the withdrawal agreement called for by the UN General Assembly being held to by the parties to the dispute—the Israelis, French, British and Egyptians—and they didn't depart from it. You didn't have any serious break in the overall position, although the Russians did challenge the validity of moving the authority from the Security Council to the General Assembly, because they always challenge that. Then you had this very efficient and considerate commander who could carry out the instructions of the Secretary-General and also get the sympathetic support of his subcommanders. So it all worked very well.

No detail escaped Tommy's attention. When he wasn't busy with the Israelis, French and British, he had time to design the entire blue UN uniform that is still used today!

By December 4, 1959, the UNEF was firmly entrenched in Egypt. All the countries involved had developed systems and protocols to deal with the peacekeepers. It was time for Tommy Burns to return home. The Canadian government asked Tommy to become the disarmament adviser to Canada. In 1960 he was appointed counsellor for disarmament issues in the Canadian government, with the rank of ambassador.

Dag Hammarskjöld, Secretary-General of the UN, praised Tommy for his success in Egypt:

> *General Burns has rendered distinguished service to the United Nations and made a significant contribution in its efforts toward quiet and peace. With devotion to the United Nations and its ideals he has helped it mould its ability to be a unique and pioneering peace force.*

Tommy Burns, the old soldier who had dreamed of war, trained for war, prepared himself for success in war, fought in two wars, and failed in war, became known to the world as the world's first soldier of peace.

In his later years, Tommy returned to writing. *Between Arab and Israeli* chronicled, in detail, the actions during the UNEF and Tommy's reasons for accepting the peacekeeping position along the Suez. He wrote:

> *I was happy in the service, and felt I was pursuing an honourable profession, and was sustained by the philosophy that war, however regrettable many of its features, was inevitable in the then state of development of the human race; and that peoples who refused to contemplate the possibility of war, and indeed to prepare for it, would be likely to be pushed off the world's stage by those who still thought of war as a means of settling differences not otherwise reconcilable.*

So, war being something to be avoided at almost any cost, the alternative way to settle international differences had to be some supranational machinery for the purpose....Whatever the imperfections of the United Nations Organization, the ideal of the prevention of a war which would destroy countless million man-years of thought and labour was there, in the United Nations Charter. Everyone who believed in that ideal—that common-sense alternative to mutual destruction—had a duty to do what he could to make this aspiration into a reality....

He wrote many other books including: *Manpower in the Canadian Army, 1939–1945* (1956), *Megamurder* (1966), *General Mud: Memoirs of Two World Wars* (1970) and *A Seat at the Peace Table: The Struggle for Disarmament* (1972).

Tommy Burns's actions as a peacekeeper brought him the rewards that war did not. He received several honorary doctorates, was hailed as a hero in the media, and his rank, lost during World War II, was restored to lieutenant general.

In 1967 Tommy received, from Queen Elizabeth II, the highest degree of the Order of Canada, Companion. He was made a professor of strategic studies at Ottawa's Carleton University and taught there from 1972 to 1975. Finally, the UN awarded him the Pearson Peace Prize in 1981.

Tommy Burns died in Manotick, Ontario, on September 13, 1985. Friends and colleagues remembered him as a brilliant man, perhaps the brightest-ever Canadian officer. He is remembered both for his books and his inventions. He is also remembered as Canada's first soldier of peace, setting the standard for all those who follow.

Many retired generals, since 1945, have become convinced that western civilization could be almost obliterated if there should ever be another great war. If war is obsolete for the settling of international disputes, should the injunction of Micah not be obeyed: "Nation shall not lift up sword against nation; neither shall they learn war any more." If so, no one should teach war any more, or contribute to teach it.

–Tommy Burns in *General Mud* (1970)

CYPRUS—United Nations

Peacekeeping Force, Kato Pyrgos, Cyprus, 15 April 1964

As part of the devolution of its colonies, Britain *and Cyprus came to an agreement in 1959 giving the small Mediterranean island its independence. The challenge was that both Greece and Turkey claimed ownership of the island and both had citizens living there. By 1963 all efforts to find a peaceful resolution to the Turkish/Greek question had failed, and the two communities were in open conflict with each other.*

Soon both Greece and Turkey were threatening an invasion to protect their citizens. A small regional crisis was threatening to spill out into the volatile Mediterranean. Britain, afraid of a potential international crisis in its former colony, turned to the UN to restore some semblance of peace.

CHAPTER THREE

Colonel (Retired)
Donald Stewart Ethell
(OMM, MSC, CD, OStJ, AOE)
(1937–)

DONALD STEWART ETHELL, CANADA'S MOST DECORATED peacekeeper, was born July 1937, in Vancouver, BC.

By 1954, Ethell was almost 17 and a member of the Canadian militia. Like many young men in the early '50s, Don saw the military as a chance to travel and get away from home for a while. While on a six-week militia course, Don was approached to join the air force; he accepted. His father was angry—Don had not yet completed high school. He didn't have to worry for long. Don had "trouble" focusing on his work—and not the girls—and he returned home released from the armed forces.

In May 1956, Don was still focused on the military as a career. He tried to join the navy, but the military has a long memory, and his abortive career in the air force came back to haunt him. He was refused. Not to be discouraged, Don tried the army. The army accepted him, and he was soon on his way to Calgary and a career with the Queen's Own Rifles (QOR) of Canada.

Assigned to Currie Barracks, Don Ethell concentrated on the training that would soon make him a combat soldier in the service of Canada. Don Ethell was to become a very good soldier. However, no one could have predicted in 1955 that he would serve in 14 international peacekeeping deployments, including Cyprus, Lebanon, Syria, Jordan, Egypt, Israel, Central America and the Balkans.

In November 1956, the world focused on the Suez Crisis in Egypt, with Egypt on one side and Britain, France and Israel on the other. Don and his regiment watched as the world neared another world war. It was then that Lester B. Pearson suggested a peacekeeping force and offered the QOR as Canada's contribution. It looked like Don was to see his first peacekeeping mission.

The battalion flew to Halifax and were told that they had to be ready to go on three days' notice. The battalion realized that this was what they had trained so hard for and were anxious to head to Egypt. At the last moment, President Nasser of Egypt decided that the QOR's name and uniform were too close to the British, and he did not want the Canadians in Egypt. A communications and logistics unit was sent instead. It was a hugely embarrassing, and disappointing, turn of events for the infantry battalion.

The QOR returned to Calgary and further training. Don served variously with a reconnaissance platoon, the regimental police. He also spent time running an office and two years with the armoured defence platoon.

The military was not the only thing that occupied Don's time. In February 1956, Don married his fiancée Linda, and they settled down to military life. Don would later say that as a soldier: "You have to be married to a special type of person because the requirements of the service come first, and it can be very dangerous; and male or female, they have to understand that. It can be hard on the spouse and hard on the children."

Just to make the point of how hard a military life can be on a family, Don and Linda found themselves in Germany in July 1960, serving with the QOR with NATO. It was the time of the Berlin Wall and the Cuban Missile Crisis, and the QOR were regularly in the field—either training or responding to threats from the Soviet side. Don quickly moved through the ranks having been promoted first to corporal and then sergeant.

Despite Don being away most of the time, he and Linda enjoyed Germany, and their first child was born there. They returned to Canada in October 1963, once more settling down to barracks life.

Almost 10 years after Don's first "almost" shipping out on a UN peacekeeping mission, he finally got to go. In April 1965, Don was sent to Cyprus as a platoon sergeant for a six-month tour of duty. Assigned to the reconnaissance platoon, Don and his men often faced difficult situations, trying to keep the Turks and Greeks on the divided island from killing each other. Peacekeeping was not always peaceful.

Making a decision that the very best place for a UN observation post was on top of a hill, right in the middle of a Greek defensive position, the QOR developed a plan. An observation post was necessary to ensure that the Turks did not use their tanks against the Greeks. But the Greeks certainly didn't want UN observers in their midst. Commanding officer Lieutenant Lewis MacKenzie's plan concluded that the only way to get to the hill was to sneak in under the cover of darkness, hoping that the Greeks would not hear them, and if they did, not kill them by mistake thinking the Canadian peacekeepers were in fact Turks.

Just before the mission, Don met with Lieutenant MacKenzie (later General MacKenzie) to have the sequence of command explained. MacKenzie said: "If I'm killed, Sergeant Snowden is in charge; if he gets it, Sergeant Ethell is in charge."

MacKenzie, writing in his book *Peacekeeper*, remembered Don Ethell well: "Good young officers who become good old generals are made by good sergeants, and I had some of the best as my tutors—including Don Ethell."

Starting out at midnight, the force was ready for its "assault" on the hill that would (hopefully) soon fly the UN flag. Walking in front of the jeeps, moving forward in low gear, MacKenzie and Ethell led the way through the Greek trenches. Sleeping Greek soldiers never heard the Canadian jeeps as they moved uphill.

Half an hour of tense progress later, the UN flag was flying on a hill surrounded by Greek soldiers. In the morning, the Greek Cypriot commander stormed up to MacKenzie and Ethell and demanded an explanation. Sneaking through his lines was just "not on." The two QOR soldiers explained that, be that as it may, they were there to stay. The Greek commander—a pragmatist— realized he was beaten and stayed for breakfast.

Returning from Cyprus, Don was assigned to Victoria, BC. While there he was informed he was to be sent to Ottawa to work as a systems analyst at National Defence Headquarters. He really did not want to go as he preferred fieldwork, but in the military it is never wise to question an order— especially when one's career is involved. In February 1969 Don and his family moved to Ottawa for what was to be a short-term assignment—it lasted until July.

The history of the Canadian Armed Forces is one of constant evolution. Following the various unit histories—which merged with which—is a historian's nightmare. In 1970 the Canadian government ordered that the QOR of Canada be removed from regular army service and reformed as a militia (part-time) unit. Those members of the QOR who wanted to stay on as career soldiers would have to find a new home—in a new unit. Don's new home was Princess Patricia's Canadian Light Infantry (PPCLI).

October 1970 saw Don returning to Cyprus for another six-month tour of peacekeeping—this time as battalion intelligence officer. Writing later about his experiences, Don explained:

> *The missions you don't hear about are the ones that are considered "successful." This is when troops are doing their job, providing stability while knowing the chances of a political and diplomatic solution are remote. This is what has happened in Cyprus. UN Forces have been there since 1964, and the chances of a diplomatic solution are slim to none. So they maintain the status quo.*

In any army in the world, one of the most difficult things to achieve is for an enlisted man to become an officer. Good sergeants often remained just that—good sergeants. The usual route for someone to become an officer was to come through one of the military colleges. Don bucked the trend. He was informed that he was to be considered for promotion to lieutenant, but that he would have to attend night school to raise his education to an acceptable standard. In 1972 Don became Lieutenant Ethell, an officer raised from the ranks.

The Canadian Armed Forces are like any other—hierarchical and bound by rules. Posted to the Canadian Forces Officer Candidate School as an instructor with the rank of captain in May 1974,

Don believed he would end his career there as many others had. However, Don was allowed to remain a staff officer with Brigade Headquarters. In this position he continued his own studies and competed with other officers on an equal footing.

Every officer hopes to lead troops—it is what they train for and what they dream of. Armies around the world have other ideas for their officers. Any officer who is destined for senior positions must learn how an army works—not just how it fights.

In June 1976, his tenure at the Officer Candidate School completed, Don was about to learn how the Canadian army worked. He was assigned to the Calgary Headquarters 1st Canadian Brigade Group as a staff officer. In his mind he was "pushing paper," but to the army he was learning how to be a senior officer.

The training as a staff officer paid off. Don was promoted to major and then lieutenant colonel while serving with the PPCLI.

Don was in the right place at the right time. There had been 13 UN and peacekeeping missions between 1945 and 1978. For the next 10 years there were no UN missions at all. However, in 1987 the UN resumed its peacekeeping activities with many more nations asking for UN peacekeeping assistance. It would be an active time for a career soldier in the service of the country that invented modern peacekeeping.

The United Nations Truce Supervisory Organization (UNTSO) was established in 1948 to supervise
the Security Council's truce that ended the first
Arab-Israeli War. UNTSO is responsible for territory
in Egypt, Israel, Jordan, Lebanon and the Syrian
Arab Republic and the peacekeepers are required to
keep up with the changing politics in the entire
region. It was to UNTSO that Don was posted in
May 1984 as senior Canadian military observer.

As though this was not enough responsibility for
the lieutenant colonel who came up through the
ranks, Don was also seconded to the United
Nations Observer Force (UNDOF) as deputy chief
of staff with specific duties as senior liaison officer
between the UN and the Syrian and Israeli armies.

The UNDOF was established in 1974 on the
Golan Heights up to 1982 to maintain the ceasefire
between Israel and Syria. On June 28, 1984, Don
took part in one of the stellar events of his career.
The wars and conflicts that had engulfed the Middle East resulted in not only death and destruction
but also prisoners of war. Israel, Egypt, Syria, Jordan and Lebanon had developed ways of dealing
with each other. However, not all prisoner
exchanges were simple. During the Galilee war,
the Syrians returned to Israel three soldiers, three
civilians, and the bodies of five soldiers. The Israelis
returned to Syria 291 soldiers, 13 civilians and the
bodies of 74 soldiers.

Ethell, as the senior liaison officer, was tasked with facilitating the exchange once UN assistance had been requested. He travelled back and forth, criss-crossing the ceasefire lines on the Golan Heights, while trying to negotiate an agreement for the exchange between the Syrians, the Israeli's and the International Red Cross. Ultimately, the exchange was a success, completed in less than 36 hours, despite the fact that both sides were still at war.

In June 1987, Don was called back to Ottawa to serve at National Defence Headquarters as a full colonel. He was made the director of peacekeeping operations (DPO) at a time when Canada had greatly increased its international peacekeeping commitments. Canada now had forces in Afghanistan, Pakistan, Iran, Iraq, Namibia and Central America. Don was responsible for monitoring on-going missions, planning, preparing and implementing all operational, personnel and logistics activities in support of Canadian forces around the world. He also made frequent trips to UN headquarters in New York to negotiate Canada's on-going commitment to peacekeeping.

In 1988 the United Nations Peacekeepers as a group won the Nobel Peace Prize for their work around the world. Don, the professional soldier and peacekeeping veteran was less than impressed. He remembered his return to Ottawa to take on his new duties:

I was called back to Ottawa when I was in the Middle East and flew into Toronto from Frankfurt. I had just come out of Beirut and the Camp Wars, where on a quiet night only 100 people were killed. I got back to Canada and really nobody gave a damn because I remember the front page story of the newspaper that day was how many pairs of shoes the Prime Minister's wife had.

As Canada increased its commitment to the UN Peacekeeping Forces, it found itself farther and farther afield. The UN was proposing a peace-keeping force in Central America to end a series of civil wars in the region, and Canada was in full support. While still at National Defence Head-quarters, Don was tasked with meeting with senior military and political leaders in Central America to brief them on the merits of peacekeeping and to convince them to accept a UN presence on an on-going basis.

When the UN needed someone to go to the countries involved in the Arias Peace Plan, Don Ethell was seconded to the UN by the Canadian Armed Forces. After completing an in-depth analysis of the situation, Don submitted an initial operations plan for the UN peacekeepers who would be operating in Central America. The plan was accepted by the UN and supported by the Conservative government in Canada.

The United Nations Observer Group in Central America (ONUCA) operated in five countries but especially in Nicaragua. The peacekeepers with ONUCA ensured that the Nicaraguan rebels (the Contras) did not receive foreign military assistance, also ensuring the non-use of one territory for attacks on others and demobilizing the rebels.

Ethell had completed his work in Central America but not in the Middle East. In the summer of 1990, Don returned to the Middle East as chief of liaison systems for the Multinational Force and Observers (MFO) to monitor the peace treaty between Israel and Egypt.

The new posting brought a side benefit to Don. Linda was allowed to join him in the desert. They often travelled together to Cairo and Tel Aviv as part of his duties. However, their short time together in the desert ended with the beginning of the Persian Gulf War and the Canadian government ordering all dependants, including Linda, home.

With the end of the Persian Gulf War in 1991, Don was named the Chief of Staff (COS), Deputy Force Commander of the Multinational Force and Observers (MFO). Don once again was in the right place at the right time for a career military officer. Because of a bureaucratic mistake, the U.S. officer, who would normally have held the position of chief of staff, was unable to assume the post, allowing the Canadian officer to hold the job for five months. There was an added bonus. With the end of hostilities Linda was allowed to rejoin Don, and they made up for the time they missed when Linda had been sent home.

In late 1991 Don was finally replaced, and he and Linda returned home. Don had reached the magic age of 55—mandatory retirement from the Canadian Armed Forces. The Ethells looked forward to settling down to a "normal" life after years of serving in the world's hotspots.

Normal is, of course, relative. In December, less than a month after starting his retirement leave, the phone rang at the Ethell house. It was Don's career officer, saying, "You've failed retirement; we want you to go to Yugoslavia for six months." Don was not "just going to Yugoslavia" He was to be the Canadian Head of Mission with the 300-member European Community Monitoring Mission (ECMM) in Yugoslavia.

Yugoslavia was a region of the world that was politically and militarily unstable from before World War I. In fact, it was the assassination of Archduke Ferdinand in Sarajevo that sparked "the war to end all wars—World War I."

In 1992 it was not Germany and Britain who were fighting in the Balkans but principally the Serbs and the Croats who were locked in a brutal civil war. However, there were enough conflicts for everyone. Both NATO and the UN, over time, tried to monitor and control the situation. The face of peacekeeping was changing. It was no longer enough just to monitor peace, it was now necessary to enforce or even create peace. However, in early 1992, the UN was not ready for its new role of "peacemaker" and turned to NATO and the ECMM to try to stop the killing.

While Don tried to monitor and enforce the various ceasefires that punctuated the Balkans conflict, the UN began to move into the region. According to Don, the situation even "started to settle down." Then the situation went from bad to worse. In April 1992 ethnic tensions, strained to the breaking point, erupted into civil war when Bosnia and Herzegovina declared independence from Yugoslavia.

Ultimately, the civil war in Yugoslavia would see thousands die and more than a million men, women and children displaced from their homes. Each side seemed to focus on increasing the levels of violence and depravity they committed on each other and civilians. Don later said:

> It was a period of time when many of us wit-
> nessed atrocities much worse than any we had seen
> in our previous service. It was a very tension-filled
> time. I am sure a number of our members suffered
> from post-traumatic stress disorder (PTSD). It was
> an interesting time, but it was very stressful.

One peacekeeper who Don knew experienced, in one day, four cases of rifle, machine gun, artillery, and mortar fire directed toward his clearly-marked patrol vehicle.

To punctuate the horrors the Canadian peace-keepers endured, Don related the following story:

My fellow Canadian "monitor" had just arrived in Zagreb following his successful rescue, under fire, of 66 blind children during the Serbian advance in northern Bosnia. In an underground bunker he had also witnessed the senseless slaughter of 20 Serbian women, children and wounded men by Croatian irregulars. Although he had risked his life on numerous attempts to evacuate the refugees, he was blamed for the slaughter and was beaten by the Serbians. Following his hasty removal from the area, the impact of his actions and experiences struck both he and his teammates....

Peace finally came to the region in December 1995 with Yugoslavia partitioned into three regions. Each region was governed by an ethnic group—Muslim, Serbian or Croatian. However, Don did not see the peace for he was no longer in the former Yugoslavia.

In June 1992 Don finally returned to Canada for the last time in his role as soldier and peacekeeper. This time he did not fail retirement, and his military career came to an end on July 21, 1993.

As difficult as his time as a peacekeeper had been—for both Don and his family—his 38 years with the Canadian Armed Forces was well rewarded by both a grateful nation and the world. Three different governors general decorated the man who had originally been thrown out of the Canadian

Air Force. He received the Meritorious Service Cross (MSC) for his service in the Middle East— specifically the prisoners of war and body exchanges between the Israelis and Syrians in 1984 and the movement of Palestinian prisoners from Israel to Lebanon through Syria in 1985.

Other honours and awards received by Don include the Order of Military Merit (OMM) (officer grade) in 1982; the Most Venerable Order of the Hospital of St. John of Jerusalem (OStJ) (serving member grade) in June 2001; the 100th and 125th Anniversary medals; the Special Service Medal; and the Canadian Forces Decoration. He also received the Canadian Peacekeeping Service Medal in 2001 as well as various campaign medals.

On October 18, 2001, Don was invested into the Alberta Order of Excellence (AOE) by Alberta's lieutenant-governor. In November 2002 he was one of 25 initial recipients of the newly created Minister of Veterans Affairs Commendation.

Perhaps his most visible public honour was that he had a street named after him—Don Ethell Boulevard—in Garrison Woods, the real estate development that has sprung up on the old Canadian Forces Base, Calgary. It is a fitting end to a brilliant military career.

General McArthur once said that "old generals do not die—they just fade away." Don Ethell has proven him wrong. In his retirement, Don focused on humanitarian efforts, giving both his time and energy to CARE Canada as security adviser in five refugee camps in Kenya and Somalia during coalition forces activities.

His time in Africa had a major impact on the former peacekeeper. As Alberta's director of the International Committee for the Relief of Starvation and Suffering (ICROSS) he worked to relieve the suffering of those in Africa dying from starvation or the effects of AIDS—over 15,000 per day. In a media interview, Don explained his involvement in Africa by saying, "It's payback time."

Don also turned his considerable drive and determination to assisting those who had also served in the Canadian Armed Forces—Canada's veterans. He is the President of the Canadian Association of Veterans in United Nations Peacekeeping and contributes his time to important causes such as PTSD. When residences of the Colonel Belcher Veteran Care Centre moved to a new facility, Don joined the Friends of Colonel Belcher to assist with the challenges and successes. Additionally, Don serves as one of four committee chairs for the Canadian Forces Advisory Council, which is responsible for investigating and reporting on all aspects associated with Canada's veterans.

He also enjoys memberships in the Queen's Own Rifles of Canada Association and Princess Patricia's Canadian Light Infantry Association, Royal United Services Institute of Alberta, Calgary Military Museums Society, the Canadian Airborne

Association; the Army, Navy and Air Force Veterans of Canada (ANAVETS) and the Royal Canadian Legion.

Don provided the UN with reconnaissance experience and expertise through his consulting firm for peacekeeping operations in Haiti, Rwanda and Angola, and with the United States Special Forces. During the spring of 1994, he served as the military adviser to Price Waterhouse's review of the Republic of Ireland's Defence Forces. He also continues to serve as a defence analyst to the CBC and other media organizations.

Entering the speaking circuit, Don has become very outspoken on peacekeeping operations.

Canadians continue to make peacekeeping a central commitment. Canada's status as a middle power with no external territorial ambitions and its unwavering support of peacekeeping have earned us unrivalled credibility on the world stage. However, the drift of peacekeeping from that of being the honest broker to being one of the belligerents has severely damaged our prestige. Canada needs to reconsider the UN's drift towards peace enforcement, a type of peacekeeping which uses force, not persuasion. Peacekeeping is not cheap in money or lives. Canada must continue to participate—but not necessarily by allowing self-serving politicians and nations to shed the blood of Canadian soldiers.

Canada in Afghanistan with NATO

WHEN AL-QAEDA, THE NOW-INFAMOUS TERROR GROUP, *flew two airliners into the World Trade Center in New York City and another into the Pentagon on September 11, 2001, the world knew it had entered a new era. Terrorism had targeted not only the United States but all Western countries.*

Reaction was swift. The U.S., at the head of an international coalition, forced the collapse of the Taliban regime in Afghanistan, a regime that had supported, trained and protected the 9/11 terrorists. With the Taliban in disarray, the governance of Afghanistan was passed to the interim Afghan President Hamid Kharzai, in November 2001.

To assist the new Afghan government, the UN approved a NATO-led International Security Assistance Force (ISAF). The ISAF, NATO's first mission outside the Euro-Atlantic area, became the alliance's responsibility in August 2003 and focused on helping the new government to maintain its security and provide assistance in establishing free and fair elections, revamping the legal system and the rebuilding of the country.

In late 2003 Canada provided 40 percent of the 5000 members of the ISAF. These soldiers, while peacekeepers, were considered "fair game" by the Taliban, Al-Qaeda and various paramilitary factions. Canadian soldiers were once again not keeping the peace but making it.

CHAPTER FOUR

Robert Alan Short
and Robbie Beerenfenger

AFTER THE TALIBAN REGIME WAS DRIVEN OUT OF POWER IN Afghanistan, opposition leaders met in Germany, in December 2001 at what became known as the Bonn Conference. The conference started the process of rebuilding the country, its government and its infrastructure. As part of the agreements reached, NATO began to assemble an ISAF to work with the Afghans. Eventually over 47 countries, both NATO and non-NATO, would contribute to the ISAF.

Canada quickly agreed to support NATO operations in Afghanistan through Operation Athena. It was not Canada's first participation in Afghanistan—through Operation Apollo, Canada had assisted in the American-led operations against the Taliban regime. Canadians had fought on the ground, and over 90 percent of Canada's naval vessels had been on active duty in the region, searching for Al-Qaeda and Taliban agents.

With Operation Athena, Canadian soldiers returned to the role of peacekeeping—or at least peacemaking. The Americans, before beginning their pull out, had developed the idea of provincial reconstruction teams (PRT), which were military units tasked with being "a catalyst for stabilization, building relationships (with the local population) and enabling Afghanistan's reconstruction and development." NATO was to continue what the Americans had begun. Canada's Operation Athena, using land forces almost exclusively, was to provide engineering and surveillance support to the ISAF from its base at Camp Julien.

In August 2003, Canadian military planners sent the 3rd Royal Canadian Regiment (RCR) Battalion Group to Kabul. The RCR was made up of two light infantry companies, one light armoured vehicle (LAV) III company (armoured personnel carriers), a combat support company, a field engineer squadron, a reconnaissance platoon and a direct fire support platoon. A command and control team and other staff would also support the soldiers in the field.

Two of the professional soldiers accompanying the battalion to Afghanistan were Sergeant Robert Alan Short and Corporal Robbie Beerenfenger. Both were looking forward, once again, to serving their country as only professional soldiers can.

Robert Short was from New Brunswick, born on October 15, 1961, in Fredericton. His parents, Murray and Annice Short, also had two other children, Elizabeth and Mitchell. After growing up in Fredericton, Robert married Susan Dawn Fullarton in February 1980, and together they had three children—sons Jacob and Joshua and a daughter Clarissa.

February 27, 1990, was a turning point in the Short household. Robert enrolled in the Canadian Armed Forces, completing his recruit training at CF Recruit School in Cornwallis, Nova Scotia, in May of the same year. His next stop was the Royal Canadian Regiment Battle School in Petawawa after which he joined the 2nd Battalion, The Royal Canadian Regiment. From August 1991 to March 1992 he was in Nicosia, Cyprus, serving as a UN peacekeeper, and from November 1992 to May 1993 he was in Kiseljak, Yugoslavia, as part of the Canadian Infantry Battle Group. While in Yugoslavia he was promoted to corporal.

Like most Canadian soldiers Short's career consisted of numerous peacekeeping tours— interspersed with postings at home. In January 1996, Corporal Short was sent to Coralici, Bosnia, and while there became a master corporal. On his return to Canada in July 1996, he joined the 3rd Battalion, The Royal Canadian Regiment in Petawawa.

Between 1996 and 2001, Short took part in a number of qualification courses. He finished at the top of his class during both his sniper detachment commander course and his advanced assault pioneer course. He was qualified as a: small arms instructor; reconnaissance patrolman; basic assault pioneer; drop zone controller; basic machine gunner and Eryx gunner; as well as in basic parachuting; basic sniping and winter warfare. On December 1, 2000, Master Corporal Short was promoted to sergeant, capping off a year that saw him receive recognition as the top infantry master corporal in his regiment.

Short was an exceptional athlete. He competed in the Ironman Competitions in 1999 and 2000, ran the Prague International Marathon in 2001 and The Running Room National Capital (Ottawa) Marathons in 1999 and 2000. He also completed the Nijmegen March (Netherlands), in 1998, four consecutive days of marathon marching, each day 30 miles in length.

In March 2001, the now Sergeant Short was back on peacekeeping duty in Bosnia, returning home in September of that year. He remained in Canada until deployed to Afghanistan to fight the war on terror in August 2003.

Also deploying to Afghanistan with the RCR in the same month, was Corporal Robbie Beerenfenger, who was born in Ottawa on April 28, 1974, to Wilhelmina Koehler and Daniel Roy. When he finished high school, Robbie joined the Canadian Forces. He married Christina, and they had three children—Mathew, Kristopher and Madison.

Robbie joined 1st Battalion, The Royal Canadian Regiment on October 6, 1997, and served as a rifleman in Bravo Company before transferring to the Battalion's mortar platoon and reconnaissance platoon. In 1999–2000 Robbie was with the 1st Battalion in Kosovo, serving with Operation Kinetic. By the time he arrived in Kabul, he was attached to Para Company, 3rd Battalion Group.

Short, Beerenfenger and the other men of the battalion were posted at Camp Julien—Canada's base in Kabul located on a former battlefield. For the first time on a peacekeeping assignment, Canadian soldiers would actually have some of the comforts of home. Camp Julien cost $42 million to build. Canadian military engineers levelled the field and covered it with dirt and gravel to help drainage and ensure that any leftover mines were buried under 70 centimetres of cover.

To prevent access to the base, the engineers built thick walls out of garbage-dumpster-sized cloth and steel-mesh sand containers. A long fence of corrugated steel topped the wall—a deterrent to potential snipers. Turrets and bunkers completed the defences against enemy attack.

The Canadian military then brought in $50 million worth of temporary buildings, including a modern hospital with an operating room and X-ray machine and three kitchens that could each serve about 700 people. To finish the camp, the Canadian government spent $50 million in nearly new tents, kitchens, generators, toilets, showers and water and sewage systems.

Early on October 2, 2003, the men of the RCR were tasked with completing a security patrol to the southwest of Camp Julien, along a newly opened road that had earlier been cleared by combat engineers. The patrol route had then been "proofed" by vehicles that drove along it six times in the preceding 24 hours to make sure it was clear of mines. Sergeant Short, himself an experienced pioneer, had walked the route earlier in the day to make sure all was safe for the patrol. Because the patrol would take the men away from the base—along a trail that was narrow and cut through a number of wadi's or gullies—it was decided to take the unit's Iltis vehicles rather than the larger LAVs

The Iltis (German for weasel) was built by Volkswagen on the old VW Rabbit platform. Purchased by the Canadian government between 1984 and 1986, the Iltis offers less protection against mines than similar vehicles used by the American, French or British armies. U.S. and NATO planners warned the Canadian government that the Iltis was not suited to the tasks and risks in Afghanistan.

Such warnings were not new to Ottawa. By 1993, National Defence Headquarters had already recognized that the Iltis would soon need to be replaced. In the late 1990s, Canadian peacekeepers were patrolling the streets of Phnom Penn, Cambodia, in the Iltis but were ordered to stay within city limits. On longer trips, the vehicles were either towed by trucks or placed on flatbeds.

In Bosnia, the Canadian Defence Department provided its battalion commanders with specially purchased Land Rovers because the underprotected Iltis was considered just too dangerous. In Afghanistan, Canadian soldiers were reduced to sitting on flak jackets to gain some protection from landmines—a futile effort.

As the patrol prepared to move out, Sergeant Short swung into the passenger seat. Directly behind him was Robbie Beerenfenger and beside him in the driver's seat was Corporal Stirling. In the Iltis immediately behind them were Lieutenant Jason Feyko, Corporal Richard Newman, and Corporal Jeremy Macdonald.

The small convoy slowly headed out onto the road from Camp Julien. Soon after, the patrol turned off the main road onto a trail that Sergeant Short knew well because Canadian engineers had checked the area for mines only two and a half hours earlier.

The trail ran through a small gully and was less of a road and more of a sandy track. The Iltis' moved forward cautiously, their wheels slipping slightly on the loose stones and shale. As the small jeeps crawled along, Corporal Stirling manoeuvred the lead vehicle into the slight track left by other vehicles. Following the tracks of others was usually a safe practice—it meant the track had been cleared of mines.

Suddenly, about 3.5 kilometres from base camp, the ground erupted under the lead Iltis. Sergeant Short's jeep was thrown into the air by a massive explosion, caused by three Soviet-made TM-57 anti-tank mines stacked together to intensify the force of the blast. Weighing nine kilograms each, the TM-57 is "designed to kill or immobilize a main battle tank." The impact on the lightweight Iltis was devastating.

The body of the vehicle lay 8–10 metres away from a crater several metres wide. The explosion broke the Iltis in half, leaving it twisted and burned. The blast was concentrated on the right side of the vehicle, and the rear quarter panel on that side was gone completely. Some parts were found as much as 150 metres away.

The human toll was much higher. The driver of the Iltis, Corporal Stirling, was thrown clear and was later treated for second and third degree burns to his hands. The men in the following Iltis all received non-life-threatening cuts and bruises. Sergeant Short and Corporal Beerenfenger, however, were both killed instantly. A nearby patrol and a Canadian rapid reaction force raced to do what they could to assist the injured. Investigations later showed that terrorists had placed the mines after the last Canadian sweep—only two hours before the ill-fated patrol started its tour.

Soldiers and media alike were soon questioning the decision to use the Iltis. Both soldiers and experts believed that Short and Beerenfenger would have survived if they had been in an armoured vehicle. Ottawa defended the unarmoured vehicle as safe, but soon Canadian soldiers in Afghanistan were patrolling the dusty streets and roads in the more heavily armoured LAVs.

On October 4, 2003, 600 of Sergeant Short's and Corporal Beerenfenger's comrades gathered to say goodbye to their fallen comrades whom they considered heroes. As flags flew at half-mast, under a brilliantly blue Afghan sky, the two flag-draped coffins rested in the back of a truck. A lone piper played *Flowers of the Forest* as the last post as comrades who had just delivered moving eulogies stood bareheaded and saluted during a moment of silence.

As Sergeant Short and Corporal Beerenfenger began their final, long journey home, an armoured personnel carrier with two pipers aboard led the convoy. The two coffins were loaded onto a military transport plane as comrades of the two men formed an honour guard and saluted a goodbye one last time.

Major J.D.V. Vass, Officer Commanding of the Parachute Company later wrote of the two men:

> *Sergeant Rob Short was a consummate professional and mentor to many. He personified what it meant to be a soldier and a paratrooper, and he set the example for others to follow. He was an exemplary leader who would always get the job done*

and put the care and welfare of his men before him-self. Sergeant Short was a genuine family man, an avid Maple Leafs fan, an accomplished sniper, pioneer and a lover of the outdoors. He forged a reputation as both a gentleman and a compassionate section commander.

Corporal Robbie Beerenfenger was an excellent soldier, a professional and a comrade to many. Although relatively new to the company, in that short period he made an unquestionable impact and quickly became a valued asset to this organization. He was to receive the highest of recommendation to participate on his basic parachutist course and to remain with Parachute Company upon return to Canada. Corporal Beerenfenger was not a qualified parachutist on paper, but he had all the attributes, desires and qualities of a paratrooper. A quiet and confident professional, whose family meant more to him than anything else.

Less than a week later, Canadian, British and German troops assisted Kabul police in arresting the senior commander in Afghanistan's third largest-terrorist organization, Hezb-e-Islami Gulbudding, Abu Bakr. Linked to Al-Qaeda, Bakr was responsible for several murders in Afghanistan, including those of Short and Beerenfenger.

Short and Beerenfenger would be remembered by their comrades and the Afghans they were trying to help. Lieutenant Colonel Don Deene, the commanding officer of the Royal Canadian Regiment posthumously presented Short with the Lieutenant General J.E. Vance Award for Leadership in the rank of sergeant. The award formally recognizes "the significant leadership role played by sergeants within the regiment. As the section commander, the sergeant sets the standard for effective leadership throughout the unit, and it is upon their performance that the entire chain of command rests."

Both Short and Beerenfenger would have been pleased to know that a 60,000 square metre minefield in Afghanistan was cleared in the name of the 3rd Battalion, Royal Canadian Regiment. The project was a part of The Peacekeepers Demining Fund, a project of The Canadian Landmine Foundation.

On February 9, 2004, the famous 22nd Regiment, the Van Doos, arrived in Kabul replacing the 3rd Battalion RCR. It was the same day that Qal'eh-ye Moslem Regional School was dedicated to the memory of Sergeant Robert Alan Short. For a dedicated family man, and a professional peacekeeper, it was probably the most fitting tribute of all.

~◦✕◦~

Yugoslavia

Since the beginning of modern history the *Balkans have been on the dividing line between the Christian West and the Islamic East. In 1991 Slovenia and Croatia declared independence from Yugoslavia. After a short standoff with Yugoslav soldiers, Slovenia separated with little tension or bloodshed, and Bosnia quickly became a full and accepted member of the European Community.*

Croatia was a different story. With its independence came a full-blown ethnic cleansing. By 1995, Serbs, who had lived in the Krajina region of eastern Croatia for hundreds of years, were no longer there. The Croats, despite UN attempts at intervention, had driven them out, often by the use of horrific violence and intimidation.

Ultimately, the various civil wars of the period killed thousands and created as many as 1.7 million political refugees. The peacekeepers were there to try to maintain a peace that did not exist, and they soon found that there are no heroes in a civil war.

CHAPTER FIVE

Lewis MacKenzie
(1940–)

LEWIS MACKENZIE WAS BORN ON APRIL 30, 1940, IN TRURO, Nova Scotia. His father, Eugene, had served in World War II as an engineer, earning the rank of warrant officer first class before leaving the army in 1945. Eugene rejoined the army in time for the Korean War, moving the entire family to Chilliwack, BC, in 1952. The army was definitely in Lewis' blood.

By age 12, Lewis was already 1.83 metres but looked much older. He lied to get into the local branch of the Royal Canadian Air Cadets, saying that he was 15. Three years later, he lied again to get into the local militia unit.

In 1956 Lewis' father was posted back to Sydney, Nova Scotia. Lewis, his height again an asset, completed Grade 11 at the Sydney Academy, where he became a local basketball star. Rather than completing his studies at the academy, he followed his friends to Xavier Junior College and graduated from Grade 12.

MacKenzie decided to study philosophy at St. Francis Xavier University in Antigonish, Nova Scotia. But the military was never far from his mind.

While living in Chilliwack, he had met the girl that he thought was the love of his life. Joining Xavier's Canadian Officer's Training Corps as an engineering officer cadet would "kill two birds with one stone." Lewis could continue his military training summers, but better still, that training would be in Chilliwack. Lewis was back with both his loves.

Unfortunately, the love affair with the girl didn't last, but the one with the military did. In a move that his father termed "slumming," Lewis joined the infantry after his 20th birthday. In 1960, while still in school, he completed the practical infantry officer's qualifications at Camp Borden.

In September of that same year, Lewis joined the Queen's Own Rifles (QOR) then headquartered in Calgary, Alberta. By 1961 he was in Hemer, West Germany, at the height of the Cold War. The Canadian Government, and NATO, took the threat of a Soviet land invasion of Europe seriously, believing that if war broke out, it would be in Europe. Lewis, as a platoon commander with the 1st Battalion of the QOR, was commanding 35 soldiers who were part of NATO's first line of defence.

Already the tall, young soldier was coming to the attention of his commanding officers. Each Canadian unit had a sports officer, whose job it was to maintain the good health and morale of the troops stationed overseas. Lewis was selected to be the unit's sports officer based on both his natural athletic ability and size. The army has always felt that up-and-coming soldiers should face a variety of challenges.

The commanding officer of the QOR in Germany felt that his new sports officer needed more formal training. Lewis was sent to Aldershot in England to the British Army School of Physical Training. There Lewis met with officers of the British army who were also learning the art and skill of training soldiers to be athletes.

Lewis found it difficult. He was in Aldershot during the Cuban Missile Crisis when the Soviets moved nuclear weapons within 90 miles of the United States. British officers were very vocal that President Kennedy was not handling the crisis well. As a Canadian, Lewis could understand the British point of view—after all Canada was historically linked to Britain. However, Lewis also could see the American point of view, having lived and worked so close to the U.S.

On March 10, 1963, Lewis received a call. The Canadians were in Egypt as part of the United Nations Emergency Force (UNEF), and they were facing a critical challenge. The UN peacekeeping unit was made up of several countries—each of whom was beating the Canadians at every organized sport in which they competed. The commander requested a sports officer who could turn the losing streak around. Lewis MacKenzie was chosen for the job, and he was on his way to his first peacekeeping mission.

He landed in Egypt, getting his first-ever view of the desert from the window of the Royal Canadian Air Force North Star. As the plane banked over the landing strip, Lewis marvelled at how white it was. When the door opened, a wall of heat and light hit him. England had not prepared him for the desert at the height of the day.

As he crossed the tarmac, Lewis was greeted by a waiting Canadian soldier who had a jeep with its engine running. Lewis wanted to get his bags, but the soldier told him that someone would be along for them. It was imperative they leave immediately because Lewis had already been given his first mission, and they had to return to the base "at once."

As the jeep careened down the road, the soldier briefed Lewis on the objective of his mission. The Brazilian peacekeepers had been beating the Canadians at basketball every game. Lewis would be playing against the Brazilians in the next game. When he asked when the next game was, the soldier handed him his basketball uniform and told him to get changed.

Lewis changed, jumping out as the jeep screeched to a stop. He ran across to the basketball court and joined his new teammates just as the game got started. The Canadians lost, but Lewis never saw the end of the game. He collapsed at halftime from heat exhaustion and woke up in the base hospital. Sports training at Aldershot had not prepared him for playing basketball in 40°C temperatures either!

Lewis stayed in Egypt until October 1964, when he rejoined the QOR in Victoria, having spent 20 months in Egypt playing and winning at sports. By all accounts, the sports officer had increased the Canadians' health and morale at UNEF.

In Victoria, Lewis was given *the* dream job for any young infantry officer. He spent the next few months commanding an infantry platoon. In January 1965, Lewis was put in charge of the unit's reconnaissance platoon and was told to prepare for peacekeeping duties in Cyprus, starting in April.

On his second peacekeeping mission, this time as a combat officer, Lewis relished the challenge. Cyprus had been occupied and divided by the Greeks and Turks, both of whom claimed the island after the British relinquished their control. The two armies were separated by a demilitarized zone, the Green Line, which was to be patrolled by the Canadians. Lewis and his soldiers worked to keep the two opposing forces apart and at peace. As the head of a reconnaissance unit, protected by the blue UN flag, MacKenzie could go just about anywhere. Lewis and his platoon were billeted at an old bee farm owned by a retired British colonel. During his posting, Lewis and his driver, Rifleman Wise, drove over 5000 miles patrolling the Green Line.

In October 1965 Lewis and his platoon returned to Victoria and regular duties. But the army had plans for Lewis. He was sent to the School of Infantry camp at Borden, Ontario, to train officer cadets. Teaching was a role Lewis enjoyed, sharing his UN experience. Later that year he was again on the move, posted on a two-year exchange tour with the British army.

But Lewis didn't stay in Germany long. While posted at Camp Borden, Lewis met the true love of his life, Dora McKinnon, at a roller skating rink. Lewis was soon dating the pretty brunette who wore the tiniest of miniskirts (MacKenzie's description) and thinking about marriage. Then came the posting to Germany. Just three days after reporting to the third battalion of the QOR in Lemgo, West Germany, Lewis flew back to marry Dora. After a whirlwind wedding and honeymoon, Lewis returned to Germany just six days later.

The MacKenzies stayed for two years, while Lewis learned his craft. He and Dora enjoyed Germany together when they could. A high point of their stay was the birth of their daughter Kim, born in the British military hospital in West Germany in October 1967.

On his return to Canada in 1969, Lewis began studying at the Canadian Army's Command and Staff College course in Kingston, graduating in 1970. That same year the QORs were told they were no longer going to be a regular forces unit but rather a militia unit. Any member of the QORs who wanted to stay in the regular forces would have to change units. Lewis joined the 1st Battalion Princess Patricia's Canadian Light Infantry (PPCLI).

Lewis was to return to Cyprus for another peacekeeping tour of duty, this time in the summer of 1971. By this time he had been pegged for high command and needed to learn how a military operation really ran. Combat officers, while leading the "pointy end of the stick," were not able to see the big picture, or even the whole picture for that matter. Staff officers did. Lewis spent six months learning the paperwork end of a peacekeeping mission, a task that was nowhere near as exciting as leading a reconnaissance platoon. Lewis was bored most of the time, fought with his commanding officer and looked forward to getting home and once again commanding men.

In the summer of 1972, Lewis began his climb to senior command. He was promoted to major and given command of B Company, 1 PPCLI. He was commanding men again, but world events would soon have a strange impact on his career. In 1972 Henry Kissinger and the North Vietnamese government signed a peace agreement that brought the U.S. war in Vietnam to an end. The Paris Peace Accord required international observers to oversee the ceasefire, the withdrawal of U.S. forces and the prisoners of war.

Even though it was not a UN peacekeeping mission, Canada was requested to send observers to

Vietnam and agreed. Lewis immediately volunteered. However, as he had already been on two
peacekeeping missions, he was not allowed to go.
Keeping up the pressure, he was finally sent to Vietnam when another Canadian officer had to return
home before the end of the mission.

The Vietnam mission was a disaster. The terms
of reference for the observers were so obscure that
the international officers could do no real good.
Lewis had only been in Vietnam a few weeks
when, in July 1973, the government in Ottawa
decided to withdraw its observers. Lewis had seen
how not to run a peacekeeping mission—a valuable lesson.

With the lush jungles of Vietnam behind him,
Lewis had no way of knowing he would soon be
returning to the deserts of the Middle East. On
October 6, 1973, Egypt and Syria, backed by Iraq,
Jordan and Saudi Arabia invaded Israel. The Yom
Kippur War had begun. The conflict lasted for three
weeks, ending October 22 on the Syrian front and
October 26 on the Egyptian front. A week later,
the UN was asked to establish a peacekeeping mission that would place itself between the Israelis
and the Egyptians in Sinai and to assist in the
exchange of bodies and prisoners. The government
in Ottawa agreed to send communications and
logistics personnel to join what would become
United Nations Emergency Force II (UNEF II).

Lewis received his orders—report to Cairo by
December 1973 and report to the Canadian camp

at UNEF II. Lewis was the executive assistant to the commander of the Canadian contingent. It soon became clear that the Canadians faced major challenges. It was the responsibility of the UN to provide the equipment and materials required to sustain the peacekeepers on the front lines. As would soon become the norm on peacekeeping missions, the UN's system was slow to react and never had enough money to meet the requirements of the forces in the field.

But New York was a long way away, and it was the Canadians, responsible for logistics, who were on the ground handling requests from front-line officers. More often than not, the Canadians were forced to tell commanders in the field that they had no supplies to send. The lack of supplies was bad enough, but the policy for many governments was to send materials to their troops in the field with strict orders that they were not to be used by others. When field commanders visited the Canadian camp, they saw large amounts of Canadian government supplies, sometimes the very supplies they had requested but were told did not exist.

Lewis spent much of his time fighting with New York and defending the Canadians against accusations of hoarding, or worse, stealing UN supplies meant for soldiers in the field. He was more than happy to return home in April 1974.

For the next four years, Lewis took on several roles, always taking on more and more responsibility. Almost immediately he was sent to the

Canadian base at Lahr, West Germany, where, in 1976, he underwent bilingualism training—a sure sign in the Canadian army that the command structure had big plans for an officer. In February 1976, he was sent to Rome to attend a six-month course at the NATO Defence College. In July 1977, the hard work paid off as he was made a lieutenant colonel and given command of 1st Battalion PPCLI.

Lewis was now the army's expert on Cyprus, and he was sent back in the spring of 1978 for another six months of peacekeeping and returned to Canada in September. His experience was starting to pay off for the Canadian Armed Forces. In August 1979, he was sent to the Canadian Forces Command and Staff College in Toronto where he would remain on the faculty for three years.

Being in Canada for what is, in the army, an extended period, Lewis was able to indulge a life-long passion for car racing. In September 1981, the lieutenant colonel and peacekeeper won the Canadian Sports Car Championship for GT3 cars held in Gimli, Manitoba.

In May 1982, Lewis was promoted to full colonel and left Toronto for Carlisle, Pennsylvania, to complete a one-year fellowship at the United States Army War College. The War College is a prestigious school for military officers and senior bureaucrats who graduate with what is considered an advanced degree in political science. Lewis would later credit his training in Carlisle with helping him make sense of Balkans politics.

Returning to Canada, Lewis was again posted to several positions to enable his understanding of the nuances of the Canadian Armed Forces. In May 1983, he was at the army headquarters in St Hubert, Québec, with responsibility for army training. In the summer of 1985 he was transferred to National Defence Headquarters as Director of Personnel Career Officers, where he managed the careers of 16,000 majors, captains and lieutenants. Later that year he was appointed director of Combat Related Employment for Women, a project designed to see if women could be integrated into combat roles in the army. In the spring of 1988 he was in New Brunswick, as the commander of Base Gagetown, the largest military base in Canada and the home of the Army's Combat Training Centre. Lewis became responsible for training Canada's combat officers.

Then, in 1989, the UN faced a new challenge. This time the task was not in the deserts of the Middle East but in Central America. In November, the UN Observer Group in Central America (ONUCA) was established at the request of Costa Rica, El Salvador, Guatemala, Honduras and Nicaragua in an effort to prevent the movement of goods and personnel between those countries. In reality, the mission was to try to help stop the war in Nicaragua.

With his posting at Gagetown coming to an end in summer 1990, Lewis had the opportunity to reflect that it had been 12 years since his last UN mission. That was about to change. In April the government sent him to Spanish language school, and in June 1990, he was ordered to Central America as deputy commander and chief of staff for the UN mission, arriving with Dora in the Honduras on August 7.

Lewis was responsible for meeting with senior government and military officials to ensure their co-operation with the peacekeepers. It would be good training for a senior peacekeeper. On December 21, 1990, Lewis was named as commander of the peacekeepers on an interim basis when the Spanish general in command returned to Spain. The UN worked with its usual speed, and Lewis remained the commander until May 1991, when he handed control of ONUCA to the Spanish general who was finally sent to replace him. Lewis and Dora returned to Canada.

In July 1991 Lewis was named the deputy commander of the Canadian Army's Land Forces Central Area Toronto. He would remain there until March 1992 when he was sent on perhaps the most important and difficult mission of his career—Yugoslavia.

When Marshall Tito, Yugoslavia's leader, died, forces were unleashed that had been held in check during his dictatorship. Ethnic nationalism became the driving force that led to the independence of many of the Yugoslav republics but was also the cause of a violent civil war that was waged on ethnic, religious and nationalist lines.

When Slovenia and Croatia declared their independence from Yugoslavia on June 25, 1991, the Yugoslav National Army entered Slovenia in an effort to subdue the republic. The result was civil war.

As in any war, the causes and contributions were complex. Canada would ultimately act as a peacekeeper in a war that it had a small hand in supporting. Croatian leader, Franjo Tudjman, actively encouraged ethnic tensions by firing ethnic Serbs from public service and encouraging Croatians living in Bosnia Herzegovina to attack other ethnic groups and join Croatia. His campaigns left Serb minorities open to abuse and death. Ethnic Croatians around the world who contributed supplies and money supported Tudjman. (Many contributors lived in Canada.)

Since World War I, Europe had been wary of the political and ethnic tensions in the Balkans. After all, World War I had started in that region. As the rest of the world watched Yugoslavia break into its constituent parts, the European Union (EU) decided to use its new power and economic strength to somehow mitigate the damage. (The EU had grown in 1992 with the declaration of an open market between its members.) The EU, together with NATO, established the Economic Community Monitoring Mission (ECMM) to monitor the war in Yugoslavia.

Placing huge importance on European security in its foreign policy, Ottawa was also watching the Balkans. Canada had participated in two world wars and had been a founding member of NATO—all because it knew that a free Europe meant a safe Canada—both politically and economically.

If the situation in the Balkans degenerated into full-scale war, it ran the risk of drawing Greece and Turkey (both NATO members) into the conflict. With NATO members drawn into the fighting in the Balkans, Canada would have no choice but to come to their assistance. All-out war in Europe was definitely not in Ottawa's plans. Sending observers to the ECMM seemed like the best way for Canada to avoid having to send soldiers.

Europe began to realize that the Balkan conflict was not going to be over soon. One of the indicators was the presence of refugees from the region flooding into Belgium, France and Britain. Fearing domestic political instability from the refugees, the major three called on the United Nations on November 13, 1991. Their vision was that if the UN could deliver humanitarian aid, the refugees could be convinced to remain in the Balkans—reducing political pressures on the European capitals.

Amazingly enough, the UN managed to work with some speed. Two weeks later, the Security Council passed Resolution 721 authorizing 10,000 peacekeepers for Croatia. The UN Protection Force (UNPROFOR) was to ensure a ceasefire in Croatia. Fitting the classic model of the UN peacekeeping missions, UNPROFOR was to be a lightly armed, multinational force delivering humanitarian aid while remaining impartial to both sides in the conflict and facilitating a peaceful resolution to hostilities.

Perhaps speed was not the best answer in the Balkans. The UN made some early fundamental errors that would haunt the entire mission. The first was that the UN demanded that the head-quarters for UNPROFOR be in Sarajevo, more than 300 kilometres from where the ceasefire was to be administered. It would put UN commanders a long way from their men and at a huge disadvantage from both a tactical and logistics perspective.

Further, UN peacekeeping had traditionally hit the ground once both sides in the conflict had come to a ceasefire and had requested the UN's assistance. In the former Yugoslavia, none of these conditions was in place. The EU had requested the peacekeepers. The various factions in the civil wars simply saw the blue berets as an impediment to waging "real" war against their enemies.

However, the UN was not as quick to get men on the ground. It was not until February 21, 1992, a full 14 weeks after authorizing peacekeepers for Croatia, that the UN actually passed Resolution 743 establishing UNPROFOR and giving it permission to deploy 14,400 peacekeepers for one year. Six weeks later, the troops began to arrive—including 1200 Canadians.

The first Canadian contingent to UNPROFOR, dispatched from Germany, was mainly from the 1st Battalion, Le Royal 22e Régiment (the famous Van Doos), with about 40 percent coming from the 3rd Battalion Also a combat engineer squadron (company) from 1 Combat Engineer Regiment in Lahr, was sent to the region.

Lewis arrived in the situation as UNPROFOR's Chief of Staff. He had spent time in New York before leaving for Sarajevo, where he was instructed that UNPROFOR was only to use "such force necessary to guarantee the delivery of humanitarian aid" and establish a number of "safe havens" for the Bosnian Muslims.

It did not take Lewis long to realize that ghosts of other UN missions were in Yugoslavia. The UN had not obtained enough intelligence before committing to the mission, had not confirmed the military situation on the ground and had not ensured enough men or materials were available for their tasks. He had, unfortunately, seen it all before.

Lewis was to work with troops from 31 countries as he assumed command of Sector Sarajevo. His first few days in the city had Lewis trying to find accommodation for himself and the peacekeepers. The host country has, by UN mandate, to provide free housing for peacekeepers. However, because no one had officially invited the UN, it was hard to get anyone to take responsibility. It was a sign of things to come.

Just as in Egypt, Lewis was next faced with a shortage of goods and services. Peacekeeping missions are made up of many different units from many different countries. These forces are not unified nor do they use the same equipment. A challenge for Lewis was to match the right equipment with the right troops, right down to the different foods needed to meet the various religious requirements of the troops. All this at a time when Lewis was fighting with New York because the UN system "couldn't even keep up with [the] demands for paper and pencils."Things went from bad to worse. On March 1, 1992, fighting erupted in Sarajevo after the Serbs boycotted a Bosnian independence vote. Caught between the warring factions, Lewis later wrote that his UN force "had no mandate from the United Nations Security Council to get involved in the affairs of Bosnia, yet the situation was deteriorating all around us."

Lewis would not only face challenges on the ground but also politically. International law states "no separatist state should be recognized by the international community until the constituent minorities are satisfied with the terms of the partition or until a neutral third party ensures that the human rights of all minorities affected by the partition will be protected." Many European states, and Canada, recognized Slovenia, Croatia and Bosnia Herzegovina before any protections were in place.

Canada did not establish official diplomatic relations with Bosnia until 1995. However, by recognizing Bosnia, Ottawa created a situation where Croats, Muslims and Serbs multiplied the level of violence to increase their power, territorial holdings and ethnic cleansing.

As the situation deteriorated to all-out chaos, Lewis came face to face with a major weakness in UNPROFOR—lack of forces. He estimated that to do the job in Bosnia, he would need 70,000 peacekeepers. He had only 4000.

The second problem was that UN peacekeepers were not to carry or use offensive weapons, meaning that Lewis and the other peacekeepers were caught in an all-out war without the ability to take pre-emptive action or to effectively deal with combatants armed with the latest long-range weapons.

Canada had dealt with the issue since its first peacekeeping mission in 1956. The Canadian government was allowed by the UN to send extra supplies and equipment to peacekeeping missions for the use of its personnel, as long as Canada paid for it directly. Canada was not allowed to deduct these costs from its annual UN dues or its peacekeeping contributions. Lewis' long list of friends in the Canadian forces came to his rescue. When he requested extra vehicles and equipment, his wish list was met in full.

The UN had requested that the Van Doos, a totally mechanized battalion, replace most of its M113 armoured personnel carriers (APCs) with trucks. The Canadian commander in Germany,

Brigadier General Clive Addy, one of Lewis' friends, refused. The Van Doos arrived in Croatia supported by APCs, including those equipped with TOW anti-tank missiles and 81mm mortars.

Lewis continued his non-stop negotiations between the various factions in the war. It was clear there was no real solution to the war, but at the very least, some relief supplies needed to get through to the people of Sarajevo. Lewis came to a decision. In an effort to increase the volume of relief supplies reaching Sarajevo, the airport would open to an international airlift of supplies.

Another extended round of negotiations finally convinced all sides that the world would look at each of them in a better light, and perhaps support their side in the international negotiations, if they would support the UN controlling the airport. Finally, all agreed.

At the same time, French Prime Minister François Mitterrand made an unscheduled visit to Sarajevo, landing by helicopter but leaving by his private jet. It proved to the world that aircraft could land safely in Sarajevo. As he was leaving, Mitterrand asked Lewis if there was anything he could do to help. MacKenzie replied that the French should send planes with supplies to prove to the world that the airport was indeed open for business. The next morning the aid began to flow in, led by the French.

As the situation in Sarajevo continued to deteriorate, the original mandate of UNPROFOR began to change. In May and June, the Canadian forces that had been deployed to monitor the Serb/Croat ceasefire line were just beginning to settle. Lewis then received orders from New York that UNPRO-FOR was to open a way for convoys of food and medical supplies to Sarajevo and the surrounding countryside.

Lewis' concerns about having offensive fire-power available would now be rewarded. It was clear that only the Canadians had the APCs that would be necessary to accompany the convoy. On Canada Day, July 1, 1992, the Canadians "saddled-up" and headed for Sarajevo. The journey required forcing their way through Serb checkpoints, manoeuvring around warring factions and finally arriving at Sarajevo airport. There had been a spe-cial (and perhaps dangerous) dimension to their convoy. Each kilometre of travel was reported live to the waiting world media.

The 750 Canadian peacekeepers arrived in Sara-jevo and occupied the airport, securing it for more aid flights.

Lewis had one other weapon at his disposal in Sarajevo—the world media. He became a media celebrity by using the press to get the message out, telling the world what was really happening in the war-torn city and how well the peacekeepers were doing. Martin Bell, of the BBC, said later that, over a 30-day period, MacKenzie was inter-viewed more than any other human being in the history of television. Lewis did get the world's attention, though he would later live to regret it.

One of the primary roles UNPROFOR had to maintain was being impartial to all sides in the civil war. Because there was no formal ceasefire, this often meant that, against his better judgment, Lewis found himself doing favours for one side or the other to ensure that he could complete his mission. The opposing side would then make a request that he had to meet if he was not to be seen as "picking favourites."

Both sides used his predicament to their advantage, allowing them both to continue fighting and killing. Also, each side believed that Lewis was in fact practicing favouritism, and the death threats began. Lewis was threatened so often that he had to have a personal bodyguard wherever he went, and his credibility with the leaders of each of the factions was being destroyed. His usefulness to the mission was quickly coming to an end.

Finally, in a moment of candour and frustration, he spoke to the media one last time. In July 1992, he was quoted as saying: "If I could convince both sides to stop killing their own people for CNN, perhaps we could have a ceasefire." It was taken out of context, but it truly meant the end of his role in Yugoslavia.

Lewis was ordered to return home. Everyone knew it was unfair, but such was international politics. However, Lewis was a general from the old school. He had made a promise to the Canadian soldiers that he would not leave Sarajevo until the last one of them had. Using his contacts, both in Yugoslavia and in Canada, he delayed his departure to coincide with the return of the Van Doos to Croatia. As they left their duties at the airport in Sarajevo, Lewis was there, shaking the hand of each one. When they drove off, Lewis was ready to go home.

Back home, Lewis was appointed commander of the army in Ontario, and in 1993, won the prestigious Vimy Award from the Conference of Defence Associations Institute.

However, the conflict in the former Yugoslavia followed Lewis back to Canada. He was accused of war crimes, both by members of the Croatian community in Canada and in Bosnia. He tried to defend himself but felt it was impossible because, as a military officer, he could not speak out publicly on government policy. He finally retired from the military in March 1993, after criticizing the UN's inability to effectively control or even support its peacekeepers in the field.

Lewis' book on his time in the Canadian Armed Forces, *Peacekeeper: The Road to Sarajevo*, became a bestseller and was turned into a documentary, *A Soldier's Peace*, that has been aired in over 60 countries. The film won a New York Film Festival award in 1996.

CHAPTER SIX

Mark Isfeld, Engineers
(1962–1994)

MARK ROBERT ISFELD WAS BORN ON AUGUST 14, 1962. THE native of Chilliwack, BC, joined the Canadian Armed Forces and served in 1 Combat Engineer Regiment (1CER) Canadian Military Engineers, including three peacekeeping missions—two in Yugoslavia and one in Kuwait. Mark was an expert on demining operations—removing the landmines that killed and maimed thousands of solders and civilians alike around the world.

In 1991, Mark Isfeld was in Kuwait working on demining operations after the Gulf War. He was also working on wedding plans—long distance. His fiancée, Kelly, from Everson, Washington, insisted on a summer wedding. Mark, the practical soldier, insisted on a Christmas wedding because it was the army's policy to get men home for the holidays whenever possible. Mark knew that a Christmas wedding date would mean more anniversaries spent together.

The following year, Mark was posted to Croatia on peacekeeping duties—sweeping for mines near Camp Polom. He was less than impressed with what he saw. In letters home to family and friends he wrote:

From my eyes, Croatia is a terrible scar on a once-beautiful face. I have seen churches possibly 500 years old in ruins. A monastery with breath-taking architecture; fruit trees and grapevines fill a courtyard where human voices are gone. I can almost imagine priests gathering grapes to make wine for their communion. The church has a tall steeple with a stunning mosaic on the front. A clock hangs from the other side, but time has stopped for this ancient, sacred place of worship.

Isfeld's previous posting in Kuwait was very different from the one in Croatia. He wrote:

While in Kuwait I got a little tired of shaking hands and waving to the civilians. In Kuwait, people understood that we were there to help and protect them. Often, as we travel through the [Croatia] countryside, people shake their fists or give us a well-placed centre finger. At first I was a little bitter, this was not the reaction I am used to or expected.

His letters continued:

In Croatia, where no one trusts soldiers of any sort, they see us as some sort of trouble, but I will keep on doing my duty of protecting nations that wish for peace. I will risk my life daily using the special skills I have been given by my country to help keep civilians and UN soldiers safe in travel and daily function.

Mark was never far from the reality of his job. When he was not in the field finding and defusing mines, he was teaching his fellow soldiers about the dangers the explosive devices posed. Travelling between military checkpoints, he emphasized that one engineer had already been killed by landmines and a corporal in the infantry had lost a foot. The explosives killed indiscriminately.

In October 1992 an old friend, Andrew Holota, visited Mark in Croatia. Mark complained to him about being separated from his unit—1 Combat Engineer Regiment (1CER) then stationed in Daruvar. Mark and his section had been attached to Princess Patricia's Canadian Light Infantry (PPCLI).

Isfeld started referring to his unit as "The Lost Boys Two." Lost Boys One had been what 1CER had called themselves when they were posted to Kuwait, by the Canadian government, without the basic equipment or shelter they needed.

Many of Mark's fellow soldiers hated their time in the former Yugoslavia. The soldiers were repulsed by the senseless killing and destruction and wondered, often out loud, why they were even there. The common soldiers name for Yugoslavia was "a hell-hole." Mark did not share the sentiment— he never lost sight of the goals of the Canadian peacekeepers.

When dealing with explosives, Mark was every inch the professional. He made a point of studying every known explosive device that the soldiers and militias in Croatian were using. He could dismantle the devices without difficulty. Like most combat engineers, he was absolutely confident in what he did and how he did it.

Writing after his return to Canada, Holota related a quiet evening in Croatia:

As Mark and I talked one night in his tent, he dug under his cot and brought out an evil-looking, home-made bomb. He had found it and defused it, and as he handed it to me, he said that's what the people of Croatia are doing to each other. They are so twisted in their hatred that even civilians make explosives and booby-traps, taking the lives of women and children.

Holota was taken with the strangeness of the situation. Mark Isfeld, the tough combat engineer was talking about devices that could and did take the lives of innocent men, women and children. While he was holding the deadly device in his hand, the unit's mascot, a kitten rescued by the engineers, slept contentedly on his bunk.

Isfeld also took a great interest in the children who were a constant around the Canadian camp. His mother, Carol, made small woollen dolls that Mark gave to any child he met. The tradition started in Kuwait, and Mark and Carol saw no reason why it should not continue in Croatia. Together, the two made and distributed hundreds of dolls.

On June 21, 1994, Mark was on duty near Kakma, Croatia. The combat engineer was walking beside an armoured personnel carrier (APC) escorting the vehicle as it moved past a berm of land. Mark was watching for explosive devices that might disable or destroy the APC. What he didn't see was the tripwire that the APC hit, detonating an anti-personnel mine. The berm trapped the explosion and Mark took the full force of the blast.

Captain John M. Organ, the padre for 1PPCLI, was in his Iltis (Jeep) when the radio call came through. Men were down and injured. He ordered his driver to race back the 50 kilometres to the unit medical station (UMS). When he got to the gate, the soldier on duty said that a helicopter had just arrived with a casualty. Organ and his driver covered the last few hundred yards to the UMS in a few seconds.

The UMS was a modular tent, and the two battalion medical officers and the medics were working frantically on Mark and Sergeant James, who was also injured in the blast. But Mark's injuries were so serious that the resources at the UMS would not be enough to save him. He had to be evacuated to a real hospital with a surgical ward.

The medics placed Mark on a stretcher and moved him out to a helicopter waiting to take him to the forward surgical unit (FSU) operated by the Czech contingent to the peacekeeping mission in Knin. Organ stopped the medics and made the sign of the cross on Mark's forehead while saying a silent prayer.

Mark was not conscious, but was breathing with the help of a ventilator. As he was being secured in the helicopter, a doctor, Lieutenant Smith, climbed on board and settled into the seat. Smith leaned out of the helicopter and told Organ, "John, I think you should head to Knin as well." Organ returned to the UMS, visited with the other injured men and then got into his Iltis, telling his driver to head for Knin as quickly as possible.

When Organ got to the FSU, he could tell immediately it was the worst possible news. Smith met him and confirmed that Mark "did not make it." Smith was shaken, he had done his best to save the peacekeeper, but the damage from the mine had been too great. Master Corporal Mark Isfeld died on June 21, 1994, at the age of 31.

Mark was of Icelandic heritage; his ancestors were the mighty Vikings. Soldiers have their own ways of saying goodbye to fallen comrades. The Canadians built a replica Viking ship complete with sails, oars and a figurehead. Solemnly, the men who had stood and fought beside Mark set the longboat on fire. Symbolically, Mark left this world the way he had lived, an honoured Viking warrior, his spirit sent to Odin's Table in Valhalla.

Mark Isfeld's body was returned to Canada and he was buried in Little Mountain Royal Canadian Legion Cemetery, Chilliwack, BC.

Mark Isfeld's spirit does not just live on in Valhalla. After his death, the men of 1CER ensured that he would live forever by handing out the newly christened IZZY dolls to children wherever they serve. The tradition has spread and is now a symbol of Canadian peacekeeping around the world.

Mark Isfeld, and the Canadian Military Engineers, were profiled in a National Film Board of Canada documentary *The Price of Duty*. The film premiered in Calgary in June 1995 and chronicled the dangerous work of the engineers in the Balkans and the ultimate price Mark paid for his country.

In October 2001, Mark R. Isfeld Secondary School in Courtenay, BC, was officially named in Mark's honour.

The Canadian Landmine Foundation also honoured Mark's memory. According to their website: "a minefield is being cleared in Master Corporal Isfeld's name in Croatia near where he was killed. The 27,000 square metre minefield is located in Bila Vilka village. The area is contaminated by mines and includes homes, a local playground, and a portion of the Vuksic-Bila Vlaka Stankovci road belt. The area was severely affected by the war, and most of the population has returned despite the threat of landmines. This mine action project is vital to the safety of the men, women and children who live in the area." It would have made Mark proud.

In a letter written to a friend, shortly before his death, Mark wrote:

> *I know what this stuff* [landmines] *can do—civilians, small children don't. My skills are to protect them. Engineers think of how many lives they are saving, not of the one they risk.*

~❦~

CHAPTER SEVEN

Thomas Hoppe

MARK ISFELD IS NOT THE ONLY CANADIAN HERO WHO served on peacekeeping duties in the former Yugoslavia. Sergeant Thomas Joachim Hoppe was a Vancouver native serving with Lord Strathcona's Horse Royal Canadians when he was sent on his peacekeeping mission to Yugoslavia.

Sergeant Hoppe had a busy six-month tour of duty. July 1994 found him commanding an observation post in Bosnia-Herzegovina and located between the warring Muslim and Serb factions. The observation post was flying a UN flag and should have been safe from combatant fire. It should have been, but in the former Yugoslavia, the rules just did not apply.

The Canadians were often under direct fire, with the command post taking incoming rounds from both small arms and anti-tank weapons. Hoppe later reported that the fire was both directed and well aimed. In July, the position became untenable. Hoppe knew that he would have to move his men to safety, and quickly. Withdrawing from an observation post under intense fire is both dangerous and difficult.

Hoppe ordered his men to return fire to buy him some time to begin the evacuation. Later his men said that he was calm and controlled as he directed the movement of both men and machines to safety. He received the Meritorious Service Cross (MSC) for his exceptional leadership.

Sergeant Hoppe was not finished. On August 30, he was on patrol near Visoko, Bosnia, where snipers were a constant threat, and the Canadians had learned to keep their heads down when they moved on the streets in their armoured personnel carriers (APCs).

Soon, Hoppe recognized the familiar sound of sniper fire. Looking around him he tried to see either the snipers or their targets. In moments, he saw the targets, three young children hiding behind the gates of a cemetery, trapped by the bullets impacting around them.

Hoppe jumped out of the APC on the side away from the snipers. Protected, for the moment by the heavy armoured vehicle, he ordered the driver to manoeuvre as close as he could to the boys. The driver did what he could, forcing his way toward the cemetery gates with Hoppe running beside the vehicle. However, the driver could not get all the way to the trapped children.

Recognizing that the APC had gone as far as it could Hoppe broke cover and sprinted towards the boys. The fire was intense as three snipers tried to target the Canadian sergeant. Hoppe dove behind the gates, now sharing the shelter with the three boys.

He knew they had to get out quickly if any of them was to survive. Breaking cover again, he pushed and pulled the boys toward the APC. As sniper rounds slammed into the ground, and debris around him, he practically threw the boys into the open doors of the APC, and its protective armour skin.

Sergeant Thomas Hoppe received the Medal of Bravery (MB) and the gratitude of three small boys, for his actions that day. In just 30 days, Hoppe became the only Canadian soldier since World War II to win both the MSC and the MB.

Thomas Hoppe retired from the military and is now living near Kingston, Ontario. His battles now are for the rights of Canadian military veterans.

CHAPTER EIGHT

The Soldiers of the Medak Pocket

CANADIAN PEACEKEEPERS IN THE FORMER YUGOSLAVIA FACED many challenges during their 18 months in the country. On the surface, the task was simple. Separate the various combatants and disarm them. The reality was much different. The Canadians faced disorganized and poorly disciplined "soldiers" who were much more interested in slaughtering civilians and ethnic cleansing than they were in following the niceties of international peacekeeping arrangements.

The worst area in the country, if that can be determined, was the mountainous region of Croatia called Vjona Krajina, or military frontier. The area had long been isolated, even by the standards of Yugoslavia and was the home of 500,000 extremely nationalistic Krajina Serbs. For the Serbs, the civil war was the perfect excuse to drive out the Croats who lived in the region.

On September 9, 1993, Croatian commander Rahim Ademi launched an attack on the Medak Pocket with the objective of capturing the Serb-controlled territory. There were 400 Serbs living in the area, and the UN was worried they would be slaughtered by Ademi's forces. The UN turned to its forces on the ground and ordered Canadian peacekeepers to the area.

Canada had agreed, 18 months earlier, to provide troops to the United Nations Protection Force (UNPROFOR) in the former Yugoslavia. The Canadian troops were typically sent on six-month long tours of duty, and in September 1993, the responsibility fell on the 2nd Battalion, Princess Patricia's Canadian Light Infantry (PPCLI).

The PPCLI were five months into their six-month tour of duty. Normally, Lieutenant Colonel James Calvin and his force of 875 would have been looking forward to going home. Instead, they were thrown into one of the most volatile and dangerous regions in the world. Colonel Calvin's force was a mixture of both regular force and reserve soldiers. In fact, 70 percent of the Canadians in the Medak Pocket were reservists. Calvin was most concerned. While reservists had no shortage of courage, their training was not as extensive or comprehensive as regular soldiers.

Yet, Calvin was sure they would perform well. They'd had four months of active duty in the region, his platoon leaders were seasoned and professional, and two mechanized companies of French troops supported the troops of 2 PPCLI.

Colonel Calvin knew that the task in the Medak Pocket would not be like the peacekeeping missions envisioned by Lester Pearson in the 1950s.

In the Medak Pocket, the ability to negotiate with combatants who wanted peace would be replaced with traditional infantry combat and survival skills.

The 2 PPCLI had an ace up its sleeve. The UN discouraged international peacekeepers from using weapons that could be considered "offensive" but did allow individual countries to make their own final decisions. The Canadians had always taken advantage of the loophole and sent its full complement of weapons with its peacekeepers.

The Canadian troops were protected by M-113 armoured personnel carriers (APCs), which had .50 calibre machine guns, the gunner protected by thick armour. They had brought with them C-6 medium machine guns and 84 mm Carl Gustav anti-tank rocket launchers. The men carried C-7 automatic rifles, based on the American M-16, and platoons were supplied with C-9 light machine guns.

When Canada first sent troops to UNPROFOR in 1992, General Lewis MacKenzie demanded that not only should the men have the best, but they should also have a larger offensive capability. Because of MacKenzie's stance 2 PPCLI could count on its support company with 81 mm mortars and TOW (Tube-launched, Optically-tracked, Wire-guided) anti-armour guided missiles mounted in armoured turrets aboard purpose-built APCs.

UN headquarters in New York had not been pleased when the Canadians sent so much offensive firepower to a peacekeeping mission. They felt that the combatants would get the message that the UN was there to fight, not observe. In Yugoslavia, reality would soon hit home. With no peace to maintain and with all sides seeing the UN peacekeepers as legitimate targets, the Canadian equipment was the envy of the other peacekeepers in the country.

The Canadians moved into the region and occupied a two-storey concrete building on the outskirts of Medak. The morning of September 9 dawned bright and sunny, giving no indication of the day that was to come. The men went about their daily tasks, preparing for another day in volatile Medak. Just then, all hell broke loose.

Medak came under an intense artillery bombardment. Lieutenant Tyrone Green, a Vancouver native and the commanding officer of 9 Platoon, grabbed his helmet and sprinted to his APC parked outside the front door. As he headed to the protection of the APC's heavy armour, a shell exploded in a nearby ditch and knocked him off his feet. Checking himself out, he found he was unhurt but that four other soldiers were. Luckily none was killed.

Green spoke with Lieutenant Colonel Calvin who was also unclear as to what was happening. They both recognized that to survive they were going to need real information, fast. Sergeant Rudy Bajema was tasked with setting up an observation post just outside the village of Vrebac and relaying information back to the Canadian base.

Lieutenant Green returned to the platoon's quarters, and together with the 25 men in his command, spent the next 24 hours sheltering in the basement and carefully logging each shell that fell in the platoon's battle diary. The final count was more than 500 shells hitting within 400 metres of their makeshift fortress, one only about 10 metres from the front door.

From his observation post, Sergeant Bajema used long-range binoculars to track the movement of over 2500 Croatian troops. He radioed back to Lieutenant Green that the troops were supported by tanks, artillery and rocket launchers. He also reported that a major assault was underway. For five days, he stayed at his post as the Croatians sealed off the area bounded by Medak through the Maslenica Bridge to the Maranji crossing site—the Medak Pocket.

When Lieutenant Green heard from Bajema, he sent the information to C company HQ; they in turn forwarded the information to Calvin at the battle group headquarters in Gradac. After reviewing the information, Calvin sent it by fax to UN headquarters in New York.

On September 12, the Serbs had pushed back against the Croatians and were holding them from advancing. After the Serbs dropped a FROG-7 missile into a Zagreb suburb, UN officials finally got both the Croatians and the Serbs to sit down and agree to a ceasefire. The Croatians agreed to withdraw from the Medak Pocket, and the Canadians were ordered to occupy the positions abandoned by the Croats, establishing a buffer zone between the two opposing forces.

Calvin did not trust the Croats but followed his orders. C company received orders that at 1:30 PM on September 15, they were to establish a crossing point on the main road. D Company and a French mechanized infantry company prepared to cross behind C Company and move into the former Croat positions.

That was the plan. As soon as C Company moved onto the road, they took on incoming fire.

Green and Calvin had discussed the possibility that, with the chaotic conditions in Medak, there was every possibility that the front line Croat troops would not have received word of the cease-fire from their commanders. Green responded to the hostile fire by ordering his men to put up large UN flags on the aerials of their APCs. The flags only acted as targets for the Croat soldiers.

For the next 15 hours, Croat fighters poured everything they had into the Canadian position. Small arms fire, combined with 20 mm anti-aircraft gunfire and rocket-propelled grenades, rained down on the Canadians for 15 straight hours. It was the worse firefight a Canadian unit had endured since the Korean War. At one point, the fires burning around the Canadians were so bright the soldiers wrapped their blue helmets in khaki coloured T-shirts. The Croat snipers had been using the light flashing off the blue UN helmets as targets.

The Croats were confident they could make the Canadians retreat. In the past, whenever they had taken a stand against the UN forces, it had been the UN who had backed down. This time was different. Early on September 16, the Croats made one more advance against the Canadian positions. As they charged, Private Scott LeBlanc leaped out of his trench to face his attackers. With his C-9 light machine gun in hand, LeBlanc opened fire at a rate of 700 rounds per minute. The belt-fed weapon sprayed the area relentlessly.

It seemed the poorly trained Croat fighters had never seen this before—a professional soldier holding his ground. They began to pull back. It was obvious to them that the Canadians were not going to back down. What would they have thought if they had known that LeBlanc was only a reservist?

The Croats knew they were finished; they sent word to Calvin that they wanted a truce—as they had been badly mauled—27 Croats had died in the overnight fighting and not one Canadian.

However, General Ademi ordered the Croats to keep pressure on the Canadians and the Serbs so that he could negotiate from a position of strength. Colonel Michel Maisonneuve, the UNPROFOR Chief Operations Officer and a Canadian, arrived from Zagreb to negotiate with Ademi.

Maisonneuve and Calvin went to Ademi's headquarters and found the general in a foul mood.
He yelled, threatened and raged against the Canadians, the UN and the world in general. According
to Calvin: "He looked like he was enjoying the
role he was playing. Emotions were very high, and
I was irate my men were getting shot at." However,
the Canadian's stand had achieved success. After
an hour and a half, Ademi agreed to pull his troops
out at noon the next day.

Calvin had a bad feeling. It was not like the
Croats to give in so easily. He was right; Ademi had
other plans. The Croatian commander gave orders
that his men were to ethnically cleanse the region
before the withdrawal. By 10:00 AM on the morning of September 16, the Canadians could see thick
columns of smoke spiralling upwards from all four
towns in the Medak Pocket.

Explosions and automatic rifle fire punctuated
the fact that the Croats were killing everyone and
destroying everything they could before the noon
deadline. Calvin called Maisonneuve and asked
him to get the Croats to agree to an earlier time
for the withdrawal. The Croats refused. The Canadians could not advance before noon.

Calvin was caught. His men were well armed,
but they could not possibly take on the entire
Croat force and have any chance of surviving.
Defending a position was one thing, attacking
quite another. Further, the UN was afraid that if

the Canadians advanced before noon, the agreement with the Croats would collapse. New York ordered Calvin to hold his position, no matter what.

The Canadian soldiers were so close to the killing that they could see and hear what was happening, right from their foxholes. Calvin knew how hard it was on the peacekeepers: "My soldiers knew their role was to protect the weak and the innocent, and they were absolutely incensed."

At the stroke of noon, D Company raced across the road separating them from the Croat forces. They immediately faced a new threat. The Croats had no intention of withdrawing. The Canadians were face to face with a company of Croat troops entrenched behind a barricade and surrounded by a hastily laid defensive minefield.

The Croats had also brought some heavy firepower with them. A modern Russian built T-72 tank was parked facing the Canadians, its gun barrel moving threateningly. (The tank had been a gift to the Croatians from the Germans, a legacy of the Berlin Wall coming down.) Arrayed behind the tank were two anti-tank guns that would have destroyed the Canadians light APCs. On the other side of the road was a battery of Sagger missiles.

Lieutenant Colonel Calvin walked straight up to the Croat brigadier general who was commanding the barricade. Calvin demanded to be let through as per the terms of the agreement. The Croat responded by ordering his men to cock their weapons and point them at the Canadians. The Canadians responded in the same way, levelling their C-7s.

He suspected they were stalling to gain enough time to clear away the evidence of the ethnic cleansing that had happened throughout the night. For over an hour, the Canadians held their fire. The well-trained Canadians were in sharp contrast to the increasingly nervous Croats. The Canadians were beginning to win the battle without firing a shot.

Calvin seized the moment. The international media had converged on the area when the news of the Medak Pocket action filtered out. As usual, there was a large contingent of news media, including television, waiting for the next big story. Rather than continue the standoff, Calvin held an impromptu press conference right in front of the Croat general and under the gun barrel of the T-72 Tank.

Twenty reporters eagerly took notes as Calvin detailed the fact that the Croat general was refusing the UN access and was threatening the lives of peacekeepers, even though General Ademi had guaranteed them safe passage. Calvin also detailed the atrocities that he believed were being committed by the Croats. Ademi backed down. In front of the world, he dismantled the barricade claiming it had all been a big misunderstanding.

As the Patricia's pushed past the barricade, it was as bad as Calvin feared—and worse. The Croats had systematically destroyed everything in the area. The Canadians carefully moved by burned-out buildings. The Croats had used anti-tank mines to blow up the brick and concrete buildings and had burned the wooden ones.

The Patricia's found 16 bodies, some mutilated, some burned, but everywhere they went they found rubber surgical gloves on the ground. Calvin speculated that the gloves had been used by Croat disposal crews who had picked up the bodies of more dead and disposed of them.

The Croats had even shot farm animals, dumping the bodies into the wells thereby contaminating the water supply.

Calvin insisted that the Canadians document everything they saw. The report that he submitted to the UN eventually was used as evidence against Ademi, who was then charged with crimes against humanity. When the report was released, it painted a damning picture of brutality and inhumanity. Ademi's victims included Sara Krickovic, female, 71, throat cut; Pera Krajnovic, female, 86, burned to death; Andja Jovic, female, 74, beaten and shot.

For the peacekeepers who had been in the Medak Pocket, they had been tested by fire and had passed. Four weeks later, they were sent back home to Canada to their families and to a normal life. The Balkans seemed a long way away.

However, the soldiers did not come home to a hero's welcome. In fact, most people in Canada did not even know its troops had been in a battle at all. Canadians at home were distracted. A Somali teenager named Shidane Arone had been tortured and killed by Canadian peacekeepers in Somalia, and the media wanted someone to blame. At the same time, Canada was immersed in a federal election, and neither the Conservatives nor the Liberals, each for their own reasons, wanted peacekeeping to be an election issue. The fact that Canadian peacekeepers had risked their lives in a war zone did not match the image of "safe" peacekeeping held by most Canadians.

Ultimately, the Canadians who had fought at the Medak Pocket received due recognition. In 1994 the UN awarded the members of 2PPCLI with the United Nations Force Commanders' Commendation, the first of its kind and only one of three ever awarded. The Canadian government, always slow to recognize the commitment and courage of its armed forces, finally agreed to present the PPCLI with a unit commendation. For many of the soldiers it was too little too late. Their legacy of the Medak Pocket would be the ghosts of the dead, who would not go away.

Rwanda

THE WORLD WATCHED IN HORROR AS RWANDA, A *central African country, deteriorated into genocide. In October 1990, the Rwandan Patriotic Front (RPF) attacked Rwanda from its bases in Uganda. The RPF, over a period of two years of civil war, was successful in using military force to pressure the Rwandan government. At the same time, international lenders were demanding changes to the economy and a drought further increased domestic pressure on the Rwandan regime. Its response was to arrest anyone it believed supported the RPF. Democracy was no longer a goal of the central government.*

On July 31, 1992, the government and the RPF agreed to a ceasefire and to begin negotiations in Arusha, Tanzania. By August 1993 an agreement was reached. On February 21, 1994, Felicien Gatabazi, the leader of Rwanda's Social Democratic Party was assassinated. By way of revenge, RPF supporters killed a senior government official. Government forces responded by taking to the streets of Kigali and killing several hundred people—almost all Tutsi.

On April 6, 1994, Belgian peacekeepers reported that they had seen two surface-to-air missiles being fired from the part of the city controlled by the Rwandan Presidential Guard and the Army Special

Forces. The target for the missiles was a plane carrying President Habyarimana and the President of Burundi. Both men were killed instantly.

The army and the militias had the excuse they were looking for. Soon, members of the transitional government, civilians and any Tutsi were the targets of government death squads. The killings were designed to: eliminate the opposition, eradicate the country of all Tutsi, and continue fighting the RPF.

In the end over 800,000 Rwandans, almost all Tutsi, would be dead.

CHAPTER NINE

Lieutenant General (Retired) Roméo Dallaire
(1946–)

ROMÉO DALLAIRE, THE ELDEST OF THREE CHILDREN AND THE only boy, was born in Denekamp, Holland, on June 25, 1946. His father, also named Roméo, was a non-commissioned officer with the Canadian army serving in Holland during World War II. His mother, Catherine Vermeassen, was a Dutch nurse who married the charming French Canadian soldier in Eindhoven, Holland.

When the war ended, the Dallaires were transferred back to Montréal. Wartime housing was at a premium, and the family settled into an east end H-Hut (military housing built cheaply to house soldiers) with two other families. It would not be until 1951 that the family could afford their first real house in Canada.

Dallaire was soon attending the local boys-only Catholic school, run by the brothers of St Gabriel. He was a soloist in the choir and by all accounts a good dancer. However, he was an indifferent scholar, more interested in sports than studying. There was a side benefit to growing up in 1950s Montréal, especially if one dreamed of being a military officer. Living in east side Montréal taught Roméo to be fluently bilingual.

In 1960 Roméo started his military career by joining the local Army Cadet Corps. For a young man growing up in urban Montréal, the time spent at training camps at Franhan, the old World War I army camp, simply fuelled his dreams of military glory. Dallaire dreamed of being a gunner and of serving with the artillery.

Inspired by a family friend, the avid army cadet but indifferent scholar, decided to go to military college. He was warned that with his low grades there would be no chance of his being admitted. For the first but not the last time, Roméo's determination showed itself. Studying as many as 12 hours a day, he improved his grades until, when he turned 18, he was accepted into Collège Militaire Royal de Saint-Jean (CMR) in Montréal. While at his final army cadet camp, Roméo met an elderly army chaplain who convinced him that a military career was indeed the right choice. The old priest told the aspiring officer that: "Soldiers are very unusual people. On the outside, they are the hardest, most demanding, severe people, but underneath that, they are the most human, the most feeling, the most emotionally attached people who exist." Later in life, Roméo would have good reason to remember those words.

Despite the commitment to his studies, Roméo graduated at the bottom of his class at CMR. However, he was still dedicated to joining the Canadian army, and in 1964, enlisted as a regular soldier. In 1965, he was sent to Shilo, Manitoba, to observe artillery live-fire exercises. He was enthralled. He had truly found his calling. All the years of dreaming of being an artillery officer now seemed like a real possibility.

In 1967, the military selected him to attend the Royal Military College (RMC) in Kingston, Ontario, for two more years of education. In the summer of that year, he was sent back to Shilo, this time to study to be a combat arms officer and a gunner. Roméo was the only francophone in a class of 40.

Dallaire graduated from RMC in 1969 with a Bachelor of Science (BSc). He was posted to the 5iéme Régiment d'artillerie léger du Canada (5th Regiment Canadian Light Artillery) in Valcartier, Québec. The newly formed regiment felt it had something to prove. Old line soldiers believed that the regiment, made up of French-speaking soldiers, had been formed not for military reasons but for political ones. By 1969, official bilingualism, and its controversies, was just taking hold in the Canadian forces.

The new Québec units would be tested in 1970. At the height of the FLQ (Front for the Liberation of Québec—a separatist group that believed in violence) crisis the 5iéme was deployed to active duty in Québec. It was hard for the francophone units as they had some sympathies with the motives, if not the actions, of the FLQ. Roméo was proud of how the units acted professionally in every way.

In 1970, Roméo arranged to visit the Canadian base at Lahr, West Germany. It was not a military mission. The year before, at a regimental wedding, he had met Elizabeth Roberge, the daughter of Lieutenant Colonel Guy Roberge. That dinner started a seven-year love affair that ended in 1976 with their marriage.

During a 1971 rescue mission, senior officials noticed Roméo for his efficient leadership in the field. As a result, he was selected for further leadership training. In the military, once selected, a career track is laid out—all steps leading to senior command. An important step occurred in 1974 when Roméo was posted to Lahr, West Germany, one of the few francophones to serve in a front-line unit.

Dallaire was moving up. In 1976 he was sent to Canadian Forces Base Gagetown to work on Project Franco-train. The project meant working to integrate francophones into the Canadian Armed Forces. Everything, from letterheads to standing orders, had to be translated and adopted. His success at Gagetown brought him promotion to major.

In 1978 Roméo and Elizabeth were transferred back to Valcartier, where he assumed command of a battery of artillery and 120 gunners. Command of a field unit was vital for Roméo if he was to continue to move up the ranks. All generals needed real experience. It was a stellar year for the Dallaires for another reason too; 1978 marked the birth of their son William.

With field command experience, Roméo was sent back to school. He attended both the Canadian Forces Land Command and Staff College and the US Marine Corps Command and Staff College in Virginia. When he completed the one-year course in Virginia, he returned to Canada and was appointed executive assistant to the deputy commander of the army.

In the summer of 1982, Roméo was promoted to lieutenant colonel, and his daughter Catherine was born. The new lieutenant colonel spent less than a year as the deputy chief of staff for a militia area in Montréal before returning, in March 1983, to Valcartier as the commanding officer of his first military unit, the 5iéme artillery.

Success followed Dallaire. In May 1985, his son Guy was born, and he completed his term with the 5iéme artillery. Again, the military was watching over his career. In early 1986 he was posted to Ottawa and National Defence Headquarters as a section head. A few months later on July 1, 1986, he was made a full colonel and was appointed Director of Land Requirements, responsible for all operational equipment requirements for the Canadian Land Force as well as Director of Artillery.

Promoted to the rank of brigadier general on July 3, 1989, Roméo assumed command of his alma mater—the Collège Militaire Royal de Saint-Jean. In the spring of 1991 he was again sent back to school, studying at the British Higher Command and Staff Course, Camberley, Surrey, England. Successful completion of the course saw him appointed Commander 5e Groupe-brigade mécanisé du Canada, at Valcartier, on July 5, 1991. Roméo, the son of a non-commissioned officer, now had command of 5200 military personnel and 1200 support staff.

For Canadians, peacekeeping was considered a source of national pride. For Canadian military officers, serving with the UN forces could make or top off a career. The opportunity to serve the UN came to Roméo Dallaire on July 1, 1993, when he was asked by the Canadian Government to take on the role of Force Commander of the United Nations Observer Mission—Uganda and Rwanda (UNOMUR) and the United Nations Assistance Mission for Rwanda (UNAMIR).

Dallaire was thrilled.

Imagine you are a fireman or a fire chief who spent his whole career in prevention, you'd say, "Well he did a good job, there was no fires." But imagine retiring without having gone to put out one fire or a dentist who never pulled a tooth. We had just finished 45 years of peace-time soldiering in northwest Europe...and that had just all crashed,

because of the end of the Cold War....I had gener-
als senior to me who retired without going into con-
flict, [or] *coming close to it even....And then all of*
a sudden this mission appears....It was like God
had given me finally a real challenge for my skills.
I just lapped it up. I couldn't get enough of it. And
of course, when you do get it and so many of your
colleagues don't, it creates jealousy and things like
that. But also what it does is, there are so few com-
mands like that, you're just not allowed to fail.

UNAMIR was established on October 5, 1993, by
Security Council Resolution 872 (1993). Its mandate
included "ensuring the security of the capital city of
Kigali; monitoring the ceasefire agreement, including establishment of an expanded demilitarized
zone and demobilization procedures; monitoring
the security situation during the final period of the
transitional government's mandate leading up to
elections; assisting with mine-clearance; and assisting in the coordination of humanitarian assistance
activities in conjunction with relief operations."

Dallaire arrived in Rwanda on August 9, 1993,
to take command of the 2548 military personnel
given to the mission. The mainly Belgian contingent (Rwanda having been a Belgian colony) was
supported by local military and civilian authorities.

The first action was to raise the UN flag in
Rwanda.

The place where I wanted to make the most
impact, because of the few forces that I had, was in

the demilitarized zone. So I made a ceremony,
invited both parties...[to] *a beautiful little village*
on the top of a hill, a magnificent view of the area,
and where a number of other negotiated components
of the peace agreement were signed. I wanted to do
it right there, right in the heart of the DMZ. And so,
with less than 60 troops, mostly the Tunisians...we
made a ceremony, and the significance of it in secu-
rity and so on became more and more evident as the
big wheels from the government side started to arrive
and then the big wheels from the RPF started to
arrive, with the arms they brought and us trying
to keep a certain control. It became just a mob festi-
val after the few moments of formal recognition and
speeches. But it was a great moment.

While he remained a Canadian officer, Roméo
was now "working" for the UN. He was to report
to and would receive his direction from the Department of Peacekeeping Operations at the UN in
New York City. By January 1994 it was becoming clear to Roméo, promoted to major general
on January 1, that the Hutu-dominated government in Kigali and its supporters were planning
a genocide.

Dallaire reported to New York that the peacekeepers, "...wanted to take offensive action against
the extremists who had weapons that ultimately
we were sure were to be used against us, or against
the Rwandans if the situation fell into catastrophic
failure."

He was frustrated by the lack of pre-emptive action from New York:

There was no lack of information. All the major players had ambassadors, military attachés. They knew, intelligence-wise, very well, certainly most of the dimensions of what was about to happen. There was no transfer of information whatsoever. Nothing was transferred to the UN before, during and certainly after, to my military force or to the mission in order to assist us in preventing genocide—or even during the genocide, being able to adjust whatever force I had at the time to help those who were in danger, help the humanitarian effort that was going on throughout the country.

It didn't take long for Roméo's predictions of disaster to start to come true. In the violence that started to engulf Rwanda, two political leaders were assassinated and a convoy of Tutsis, under the official protection of the UN, was ambushed. This put the UN on the defensive, a response that would have tragic consequences in the weeks to come.

On April 6, 1994, a plane carrying the Rwandan and Burundian presidents, both Hutus, was shot down over Kigali. While no one was ever officially charged, Belgian peacekeepers reported that surface-to-air missiles had been fired from the Rwandan presidential guard and special forces camps. The Hutus had manufactured a reason to start their genocide.

Almost immediately, Hutu-controlled radio aired broadcasts that called for the "extermination" of all Tutsis and the "cockroach" moderate Hutus who supported the Tutsi position. The broadcasts were specific; they detailed who should be killed and where they could be found.

What followed next was a genocide that was to last for 100 days and would ultimately kill 800,000, most murdered by their machete-wielding neighbours.

As the sun came up on the morning of April 7, the carnage had already begun. The Hutu militias, freed from any civil control, moved freely through the streets, hunting down moderate Hutu politicians and Tutsi leaders. Fearing for the safety of the Rwandan Prime Minister, Roméo sent 10 Belgian peacekeepers to the official residence to secure both it and the prime minister. The Belgians were the most experienced troops under Dallaire's command, but they were ambushed and taken prisoner. Later, Roméo found the bodies of the peacekeepers tortured, mutilated and murdered.

The Belgian government was in a state of shock. Memories of the deaths of American peacekeepers in the Somalia civil war were fresh, and Belgium was concerned it would face the same embarrassment in the international community as had the Americans. The Belgian government served notice on Roméo that it would be withdrawing all of its peacekeepers from UNAMIR.

Conditions were quickly deteriorating through-out the day. The deputy to the U.S. ambassador for Rwanda, trying to keep Washington informed, sent an official communication that the killings had moved beyond political murders, and that the militias were involved in genocide. The deputy's warnings had an impact, so the U.S. decided to evacuate all its personnel from Rwanda.

The UN was less concerned. New York ignored similar warnings that Roméo had sent to UN head-quarters. He was specifically ordered to "not inter-vene and to avoid armed combat at all cost." Roméo and the peacekeepers had to watch help-lessly as 800,000 Rwandans were murdered.

Over the next three days Roméo, still forbidden by New York to intervene, saw the nature of the civil war change. The death squads, having killed all of the political leaders, turned on the local civil-ian Tutsi population. Local newspapers reported "tens of thousands" dead and that "a pile of corpses six feet high" was just outside a main hospital.

The genocide was certainly no secret, especially to the ambassadors and military attachés from around the world who were posted in Rwanda. They had been frantically sending reports to their home countries, requesting not more peacekeep-ers but evacuation and as quickly as possible.

Dallaire and the peacekeepers were doing what they could under the direction of New York—or rather the lack of direction. Individual peacekeepers were risking their lives to pull Rwandans to safety, sometimes right out of the clutches of the death squads. He ordered that any Rwandans saved by the peacekeepers were under the protection of the UN and were to be protected. It was not the "no-intervention" ordered by the UN, but it was saving lives.

The peacekeepers were quickly running low on supplies and ammunition. At the same time, 1000 well-armed and experienced European troops arrived in the capital. To Roméo's absolute frustration, they were not there either to assist the peacekeepers or save Rwandan civilians. The troops were there to evacuate the nearly 3300 Americans, French, Italian and Belgian diplomats and civilians who wanted nothing more than to leave the country. As the heavily armed soldiers retreated to their airplanes, Roméo could do nothing but watch the aircraft disappear into the Rwandan sky.

On the ground, the death toll climbed to 32,000.

The UNAMIR was on its own, undermanned and getting no support whatsoever from New York or the rest of the world. Roméo and the peacekeepers were doing what they could. By April 15, the peacekeepers were working desperately to save the lives of those in and around Kigali. Thousands of Tutsis turned to the peacekeepers for protection as 64,000 of their family members and friends were slaughtered.

By April 16, news of the slaughter that was going on in Rwanda was being reported in the Western media. The *New York Times* carried a story that 1000 men, women and children had been shot and hacked to death in the church where they had taken refuge.

The *New York Times* might have been reporting the slaughter, but Roméo was living with it. He had dispatched men to the church in response to a call for help from two Polish military observers. What they saw was the carnage that was to mark the genocide.

According to the priest who survived the slaughter, government troops had gone door to door checking identity cards. All Tutsi men, women and children were moved to the church. At gunpoint, the troops seized identity cards from the Tutsis and destroyed them. They then opened the doors of the church and turned their captives over to the militias who had been waiting outside.

The militia, armed with machetes, started to work, bragging and laughing as they hacked at everyone. Roméo's soldiers reported that one woman had been disembowelled, her fetus hacked to death. The favourite target for the machetes was the genital area, the militiamen leaving their victims to bleed to death.

The priests and the Polish military observers begged the government troops to stop the slaughter.

Instead, the troops pushed the priests' heads up with their gun barrels so that they could not avert their eyes. By Roméo's count, hundreds died that night in the church.

Roméo was desperate. The death toll was climbing to over 72,000, and the world refused to do anything. He submitted a detailed plan to UN headquarters, asking that a rapid reaction force (RRF) be sent to the war zone. Roméo was convinced that 5000 well-trained and professional soldiers in the right places at the right times would easily intimidate the undisciplined mobs. In his words, it would "stop the genocide in its tracks." Despite Roméo's pleas, the UN Security Council rejected the plan.

Dallaire was not the only one demanding action. Human Rights Watch, the non-profit agency, demanded that the UN Security Council declare the abuses in Rwanda as genocide. In an April 19 press release, they stated that by their count the death toll had exceeded 100,000 and met all the legal requirements of a genocide, which would compel the international community to take action. The UN ignored their call.

While Human Rights Watch was making the case for genocide in Rwanda, Roméo was fighting his own battles on the ground. The Belgian government, still stunned by the deaths of its 10 peacekeepers, ordered all remaining Belgian soldiers home. The small force that Dallaire had been using to maintain whatever control he could was now reduced to less than 2000.

If that wasn't bad enough, the Belgian government went even further. Belgium was worried that if it pulled its troops out of the peacekeeping mission it would be condemned for acting on its own just as the crisis was deepening. To protect its "international image" and to justify its actions, Belgium wanted to see a universal withdrawal.

The Belgian government approached American Secretary of State Warren Christopher and asked for a full-scale pull out of all foreign troops in Rwanda. Christopher agreed with the Belgian position and approached Madeleine Albright, America's ambassador to the UN to demand the UN pull out of Rwanda. Albright, concerned that the media would condemn the U.S. and the UN for pulling out at the height of the crisis, argued that it should not be a complete pull out, just a major one.

Dallaire was also facing technical problems on the ground. As Albright and others at the UN bickered over how few men he should have, he lost communications links to his forces in the surrounding countryside. He was forced to try to retain control in a war zone with little or no domestic communications, only a satellite link to the outside world and a rapidly decreasing force of peacekeepers.

Roméo was now protecting over 25,000 Rwandans while still hoping that the Security Council would change its mind and send him the RRF while there was still time. Following the Belgian forces' withdrawal, Dallaire consolidated his contingent of Canadian, Ghanaian and Dutch soldiers in urban areas and focused on providing areas of "safe control."

The UN was not going to change its mind about the RRF. In fact, the Security Council voted to reduce the peacekeeping force to just 270 soldiers! At the press conference announcing the 90 percent force reduction, Madeleine Albright stated that the 270 men would be enough "to show the will of the international community." Weak politicians thereby imposed an impossible task on Dallaire.

The 25,000 innocents he was protecting were forcing him into a corner. Professional soldiers are trained to believe that civil authority is the highest authority there is. No soldier wanted to be put in the place of having to disobey an order. Roméo, to be true to his conscience, was faced with disobeying a legal order.

> *I was ordered to withdraw...by* [then UN Secretary-General Boutros] *Boutros Ghali, and I said to him, "I can't, I've got thousands"—by then we had over 20,000 people—"in areas under our control." The situation was going to shit....And I said, "No, I can't leave."*

The Clinton White House action was indicative of world opinion. Rather than reacting to the genocide in a forcible manner and bringing it to an end, President Clinton called on the Rwandan military leaders to "end the violence." Clinton's words had little effect. Roméo reported that 112,000 Rwandans had died since the start of the genocide.

On April 25 Roméo, still defying New York's orders to leave, watched as his force was reduced to the 270 international soldiers (supported by 200 local authorities) demanded by the Security Council Resolution. Refusing to abandon the Rwandans he had promised to protect, Roméo knew his effectiveness was now almost nil, and any successes would be by force of will alone. The dead numbered 144,000.

Dallaire knew the only hope for Rwanda was that the world community would declare a genocide and act accordingly. The Roman Catholic from Montréal was relieved to hear, on April 27, that Pope John Paul II was the first world leader to describe the situation as genocide. More importantly, Czechoslovakia and Argentina jointly introduced a draft resolution to the UN Security Council that included the word genocide. Roméo hoped the world was finally waking up to the 160,000 deaths.

The next day, the press asked State Department spokeswoman Christine Shelly whether genocide was happening. Her response carefully tried to avoid the word: "...we have to undertake a very careful study before we can make a final kind of determination...." While the state department was studying, 168,000 Rwandans were dead.

Dallaire and his few peacekeepers faced challenges on every front. The government-controlled radio station was broadcasting instructions and intelligence to the Hutu death squads. As the death toll passed the 232,000 mark, Roméo came up with an idea that might slow down the rate of killing. If he could stop the radio broadcasts, the Hutu forces would be left without a way to coordinate their attacks. On May 3, he made a formal request to the Americans asking them to block the hate messages.

On May 5 Romeo got his answer in a Pentagon memo: "We have...concluded jamming is an ineffective and expensive mechanism....International legal conventions complicate airborne or ground-based jamming and the mountainous terrain reduces the effectiveness of either option....It costs approximately $8500 per flight hour...it would be wiser to use air to assist in the [food] relief effort."

Finally, on May 13 it became apparent that some members of the Security Council were concerned, as the death toll passed 296,000. The UN members were starting to think that Roméo's plan for 5000 peacekeepers was not as radical as it first seemed. Roméo's plan called for the extra troops to secure Kigali and create safe havens in the countryside. It was risky but the best way to bring the killings to a stop.

Others, including the U.S. State Department, wanted to take a less risky path. By creating protected zones at Rwanda's border areas, the United

Nations would lower the potential of harm to the peacekeepers but the Rwandans who lived away from the border areas would be at greater risk. Ultimately, Romeo's plan was accepted. A total of 5000, mostly African troops, were committed to the conflict, and the U.S. was asked to provide transportation in the form of 50 armoured personnel carriers (APCs).

Proposing a UN resolution is not the same thing as implementing it. The African countries that were supposed to provide peacekeepers were reluctant to get involved. Intervening in a neighbour's fight might invite intervention by the UN in their own countries. The U.S. argued with the UN for over two weeks that it was the UN's responsibility to pay for the APCs and their transport.

On May 25, seven weeks into the genocide, President Clinton gave a speech to the UN. The U.S. president, known to be timid on questions of foreign policy, reinforced his view that any decision by his government to support peacekeeping missions would have to be in the American "national interest."

The speech continued, "The end of the superpower standoff lifted the lid from a cauldron of long-simmering hatreds. Now the entire global terrain is bloody with such conflicts, from Rwanda to Georgia. Whether we get involved in any of the world's ethnic conflicts in the end must depend on the cumulative weight of the American interests at stake."

The Clinton administration was clear that stopping a genocide that had claimed 392,000 was not in its national interest!

To Roméo, the genocide in Rwanda was no longer about the number of deaths or the number of peacekeepers. It was not about numbers at all. Roméo was now working to save lives one by one. While on the way back to Kigali, after escorting 200 civilians to a safe area, the genocide became very real. A small boy, about three years old, filthy, belly distended from malnutrition and covered in sores, was sitting in the middle of the road blocking the peacekeepers' path.

Dallaire realized the boy would simply become another victim if he did not intercede. Watching the sides of the road for signs of ambush he bent down to pick up the little boy. Suddenly, there was movement in the jungle. Roméo clutched the boy to him while the peacekeepers fanned out to protect their leader and his small charge. As the undergrowth parted, a well-armed RPF soldier stepped out of the undergrowth.

The soldier, only 15 years old, informed Roméo that the little boy was under the protection of the RPF because his parents had been killed. Roméo argued that the boy needed to be in a local orphanage and offered to take the boy there. The soldier would have none of it; the boy was with them.

The general and the boy soldier argued in the middle of the road, each convinced of the justice in their case. As the two were distracted, the little boy ran into a hut and disappeared. In a few strides, Roméo caught up to him and stepped into the hut. The hut stank of death, and as his eyes adjusted to the darkness, he made out the forms of the decaying bodies of a man, a woman and two children—the boy's family.

Roméo swept the boy up in his arms. "What I saw in his eyes was my three-year-old. They were exactly the same. What I saw there was a human, a human child. There was no difference there. They were exactly the same."

The UN was now convinced that the genocide was serious. A total of 616,000 Rwandans were dead, but the new UN peacekeepers had still not arrived in Rwanda. The Security Council asked France to create a safe area in territory controlled by the Hutu government. The French did what they could, but the killings continued, even in the safe area.

By June 1994, the forces assigned to the United Nations Assistance Mission in Rwanda (UNAMIR) had been significantly expanded. By July the Tutsi RPF forces were in control of Kigali, and the government forces were in full retreat to Zaire, followed by tens of thousands of Hutu supporters fearing reprisals.

The reprisals never came. More Rwandans died of disease and factional killings in the refugee camps, but the genocide ended exactly 100 days after it had begun. On June 17, a final count was made; over 800,000 Rwandans were dead.

Dallaire had lived though the worst genocide since World War II.

They were devils. And I couldn't see them as human. Just as I know there was a presence of a superior being on a couple of occasions, present as a physical vibrating sense to help me through very, very difficult moments. That same reality came through with those people. I was not discussing with humans. They had erased themselves.

Dallaire left Rwanda in 1994, a shell of the man who had arrived one year earlier. There was none of the giddiness of new command, only the weight of failure, failure to prevent the hundreds of thousands of deaths he had been forced to witness. He explained how he felt:

When you're in command, you are in command. There's 800,000 gone, the mission turned into catastrophe, and you're in command. I feel I did not convince my superiors and the international community. I didn't have enough of the skills to be able to influence that portion of the problem.

On his return to Canada, Roméo immediately went back to work. From September 1994 to October 1995, he assumed, simultaneously, the positions of Deputy Commander of Land Force Command in St. Hubert and Commander of the 1st Canadian Division.

On June 2, 1995, the Conference of Defence Associations presented him with The Vimy Award, which recognizes one Canadian who has made a significant and outstanding contribution to the defence and security of Canada and the preservation of democratic values. That same year he was named a Fellow of Ryerson Polytechnic University of Toronto and received an *honoris causa* doctorate from Sherbrooke University.

Continuing with the frantic pace, he took command of Land Force Québec Area on October 20, 1995. On January 9, 1996, he was awarded the Legion of Merit Medal by the United States. This medal honours exceptionally meritorious conduct in the performance of outstanding services and achievements. The decoration is issued both to United States military personnel and to military and political figures of foreign governments.

On July 2, 1996, Roméo assumed the position of Chief of Staff of Assistant Deputy Minister (Personnel) Group. Promoted to lieutenant general, he assumed the duties of Assistant Deputy Minister (Human Resources-Military) in April 1998.

Roméo Dallaire received the Meritorious Service Cross in 1997, which recognizes conspicuous merit and exceptional service by members of the Canadian Forces, both regular and reserve.

On February 5, 1999, Roméo was appointed to the position of Special Adviser to the Chief of the Defence Staff on Officer Professional Development.

As successful as he appeared, he was trying to control a dark secret. What he had seen and experienced in Rwanda came back to haunt him. The ghosts of the dead would not leave him alone. He had been receiving treatment for post-traumatic stress disorder (PTSD) but was not responding.

In December 1999, at the age of 53, Roméo met with Canadian Forces medical staff who told him that he was literally trying to kill himself with his work. He remembers:

> *The medical report said, it was just a very short phrase, and it said General Dallaire cannot command troops in any operation or cannot command troops in operations any more. My whole life had been commanding troops. And that's when I fully realized the impact of what Rwanda had done to me....I literally was not able to do what my whole career had taught me to do.*

The Chief of Defence staff called Dallaire to a meeting. He was informed that he had to forget Rwanda or forget the army. Roméo could not forget the faces of the dead and was dismissed, after 36 years of service, in April 2000. The official reason? Continuing health issues resultant from the stress of the Rwandan mission.

Leaving the army did not solve his problems. The faces were still there. He tried to drink himself into a stupor of forgetfulness, raged at his family and even tried to kill himself. A few months after his meeting with the Chief of Defence Staff, the general who had served his country so well in Rwanda, the man who many around the world considered a hero was found passed out, drunk, under a park bench in Hull, Québec. "He was curled up in a ball," photographer Stephane Beaudoin, alerted by a police report, later told the *Ottawa Citizen*. "I never took a photo. I felt sad for him. I thought, 'This man has done so much for us. How did he come to be here?'"

Dallaire's efforts in Rwanda were not forgotten by everyone. On October 27, 2000, he received an *honoris causa* doctorate from the University of Western Ontario, and in January 2001, The Royal Military College awarded him an honorary doctorate of military science. A year later, he was the first recipient of the Aegis Award for Genocide Prevention for demonstrating "altruism, resourcefulness and bravery in preserving the value of human life."

Internationally, Roméo was a celebrity. Conferences and think tanks around the world wanted him to speak on his efforts during the genocide. More prestigious awards were to follow. He received a Fellowship at the Carr Center for Human Rights Policy, Kennedy School of Government, at Harvard University to pursue his research in conflict resolution.

In October 2002, Roméo was featured in a documentary—*The Last Just Man*—that showed the world what the genocide had been like. In 2003 Roméo's book on the Rwandan genocide, *Shake*

Hands with the Devil: The Failure of Humanity in Rwanda, hit the bookstores and would eventually win both the Shaughnessy Cohen Award for Political Writing and the 2004 Governor General's Award for non-fiction. In 2004, he was voted 16th on the list of *The Greatest Canadian*, the highest rated military figure on the list.

Dallaire wrote the last chapter to the Rwandan genocide in April 2004. On that day, he appeared at the International Criminal Tribunal for Rwanda to testify against Colonel Théoneste Bagosora.

Roméo never doubted the mission or his command of it. When asked in an interview, after his return to Canada, if he would have accepted the role in Rwanda had he known how it would turn out his response was unequivocal:

> *Absolutely. Never ever a doubt. My whole life was to command, to be given missions, to accomplish missions—of course accomplish them with the minimum amount of casualties or destruction, and with success. I've never ever even pondered that if the opportunity was given to me again would I do it, even knowing what's going on, because I'd say to myself I'm sure I will be able to change it.*

Notes on Sources

Books

Burns, E.L.M. *Between Arab and Israeli*. New York, NY: Ivan Obolensky, Inc., 1962.

————. *General Mud: Memoirs of Two World Wars*. Toronto: Clarke, Irwin and Co., 1970.

————. *Manpower in the Canadian Army, 1939–1945*. Toronto: Clarke, Irwin and Co., 1956.

————. *A Seat at the Table: The Struggle for Disarmament*. Toronto: Clarke, Irwin and Co., 1972.

Dallaire, Roméo. *Shake Hands with the Devil: The Failure of Humanity in Rwanda*. Mississauga: Vintage Canada, 2004.

Davis, James. *The Sharp End: A Canadian Soldier's Story*. Vancouver: Douglas & McIntyre, 1997.

Granatstein, J.L. & Douglas Lavender. *Shadows of War, Faces of Peace. Canada's Peacekeepers*. Toronto: Key Porter Books, 1992.

MacKenzie, Lewis. *Peacekeeper: The Road to Sarajevo*. Vancouver: Harper Collins Canada, 1994.

Off, Carol. *The Ghosts of Medak Pocket: The Story of Canada's Secret War*. Mississauga: Random House, 2004.

Taylor, Scott and Brian Nolan. *Tested Mettle: Canada's Peacekeepers at War*. Ottawa: Esprit de Corps Publications, 1998.

Websites

http://quickstart.clari.net/qs_se/webnews/wed/ac/Qafg hanistan-canada-saf.RkfC_DO4.html

www.cavunp.ab.ca/pkofmonth/ethell.htm

www.cavunp.org

www.cbc.ca/news/background/cdncasualties

www.cbc.ca/news/background/cdnmilitary/peacekeeping.html

www.cbc.ca/news/background/dallaire

www.collectionscanada.ca/primeministers/h4-3356-e.html

www.dfait-maeci.gc.ca/ciw-cdm/Burns-en.asp

www.dfait-maeci.gc.ca/department/history/Pearson-en.asp

www.dfait-maeci.gc.ca/peacekeeping/menu-en.asp

www.edu.pe.ca/montaguehigh/grass/socialstudies/peacekeeping/missions

www.espritdecorps.ca/new_page_119.htm

www.forces.gc.ca/site/fourth_dimension/2003/sep03/09_fd_e.htm

www.isfeldbc.com

www.pbs.org/wgbh/pages/frontline/shows/evil/etc/slaughter.html

www.peacekeeper.ca

www.suc.org/news/world_articles/Toronto_Sun.html

www.thememoryproject.com/Vol3timeline.pdf

www.thewednesdayreport.com/twr/twr9/twr4v9.htm

www.thirdworldtraveler.com/Heroes/Gen_Romeo_Dallaire.html